**TEACHER'S PET PUBLICATIONS**

PUZZLE PACK
for
A Farewell to Arms
based on the book by
Ernest Hemingway

Written by
Mary B. Collins

© 2006 Teacher's Pet Publications
All Rights Reserved

The materials in this packet are copyrighted
by Teacher's Pet Publications, Inc.

These pages may be duplicated by the purchaser
for use in the purchaser's own classroom.

Copying any of these materials and distributing them
for any other purpose is a violation of the copyright laws.

© 2006 Teacher's Pet Publications, Inc.
www.tpet.com

INTRODUCTION
If you already own the LitPlan for this title, this Puzzle Pack will refresh your Unit Resource Materials and Vocabulary Resource Materials sections plus give you additional materials you can substitute into the tests. If you do not already have a complete LitPlan, these pages will give you some supplemental materials to use with your own plan. There are two main groups of materials: one set for unit words (such as characters' names, symbols, places, etc.) and one set for vocabulary words associated with the book.

WORD LIST
There is a word list for both the unit words and the vocabulary words. These lists show you which words are being used in the materials and the clues or definitions being used for those words. You may want to give students a word list with clues/definitions to help them, or you may want students to only have a word list (without clues/definitions) if you want them to work a little harder. Both are available for duplication. The word lists can also be your "calling key" for the bingo games.

FILL IN THE BLANK AND MATCHING
There are 4 each of the fill in the blank and matching worksheets for both the unit and vocabulary words. These pages can be used either as extra worksheets for students or as objective parts of a unit test. They can be done individually if students need extra help or as a whole class activity to review the material covered.

MAGIC SQUARES
The magic squares not only reinforce the material covered but also work on reasoning and math skills. Many teachers have told us that their students really enjoy doing these!

WORD SEARCH PUZZLES
The word search words go in all directions, as indicated on your answer keys. Two of the word search puzzles have the clues listed rather than the words. This makes the puzzle a little more difficult, but it reinforces the material better. Two word search puzzles have words only for students who find the clue puzzles too difficult.

CROSSWORD PUZZLES
Both unit and vocabulary word sections have 4 crossword puzzles.

BINGO CARDS
There are 32 individual bingo cards for the unit words and 32 individual bingo cards for the vocabulary words. You can use your word list as a "call list," calling the words at random and marking them off of your list as you go, or you could use the flash cards by cutting them apart and drawing the words at random from a hat (or box or whatever). To make a better review, you might ask for the definition and spelling of each word as you call it out–or you could call out the definitions and have students tell you the words they need to look for on the puzzle.

JUGGLE LETTERS
The vocabulary juggle letter game is intended to help students learn the spellings of the words. One sheet has the definitions listed on it as an extra help for students who need it or to reinforce the definitions if you choose to do so.

FLASH CARDS
We've included a set of vocabulary flash cards you can duplicate, cut, and fold for your students. Some teachers make a few sets for general use by the class; others make a set for each student. Some teachers duplicate them for each student and have the students cut & fold their own. You can cut out just the words and put them in a hat, have each student pick out one word and write the definition and a sentence for that word. Students then swap words and papers, with the next student adding a sentence of his own under the last one. You can have students swap as many times as you like. Each time the student will read the sentences written prior to his own and then add a sentence. You can cut out the words and definitions separately and play "I Have; Who Has?" Each student in the room draws a word and definition. The first student says, "I have (the name of the word). Who has the definition?" The student with the definition reads it then says, "I have (the name of the vocabulary word she has). Who has the definition?" The round continues until all words and definitions have been given.

A Farewell To Arms Word List

No.	Word	Clue/Definition
1.	ALPS	Name of the mountain range
2.	AMBULANCE	Frederick Henry joined this corps
3.	AMERICAN	Frederick Henry's nationality
4.	ANGER	___ was washed away in the river along with any obligation.
5.	ANTHONY	Catherine gave Frederick a St. ___ medal.
6.	ARMS	A Farewell to ___
7.	AYMO	Was shot by mistake by Italians
8.	BABY	It was born dead
9.	BARKLEY	Catherine's last name
10.	BARMAN	He helped Frederick and Catherine
11.	BEER	It would help keep the baby small
12.	BOAT	The barman gives Frederick & Catherine a ___ and food
13.	BONELLO	He left Frederick and Piani at the farmhouse
14.	BRAVE	A ___ person dies two thousand deaths but never mentions it
15.	BROTHERS	Rinaldi said he and Frederick were alike underneath; like ___.
16.	CAMPEN	Hospital supervisor; Van ___
17.	ETTORE	Catherine thinks he's boring
18.	FAREWELL	A ___ To Arms
19.	FIGHT	In war, one side ___s the other
20.	GAGE	Friend to Frederick and Catherine
21.	GREFFI	Frederick played billiards with him
22.	HEMINGWAY	Author
23.	HEMORRHAGES	Catherine died having ___ after the operation
24.	HENRY	Narrator: Frederick ___
25.	HOSPITAL	Place where sick & wounded people are treated
26.	ITALY	Place where story takes place
27.	JAUNDICE	Frederick's illness from drinking
28.	LEG	Where Frederick was wounded
29.	LIFE	But ___ isn't hard to manage when you've nothing to lose.
30.	LIGHT	___ For Me; horse they bet on
31.	LOVE	Feeling of Frederick towards Catherine
32.	MEDAL	Award
33.	MILAN	Hospital where Catherine was transferred
34.	NEWSPAPERS	The priest brought Frederick vermouth and ___ in the hospital.
35.	NURSE	Catherine's profession
36.	ORDERS	They must be obeyed
37.	PEACE	I was going to forget the war. I had made a separate ___.
38.	PREGNANT	Catherine's condition
39.	PRIEST	Rinaldi teases him, but Frederick shows some respect.
40.	RAIN	Catherine is afraid of it
41.	RINALDI	He was going to marry Catherine before Frederick met her.
42.	RIVER	Place Frederick jumped into to escape
43.	SNAKE	I am the ___. I am the ___ of reason.
44.	SWITZERLAND	The neutral country
45.	TRICK	I'm not a bit afraid. It's just a dirty ___.
46.	VALENTINI	A true Hemingway man; fixed Frederick's knee
47.	WAR	World ___ I
48.	WISDOM	Dear boy, that's not ___. That is cynicism.
49.	WOUNDED	Hurt but not killed

A Farewell To Arms Fill In The Blanks 1

_____ 1. Rinaldi teases him, but Frederick shows some respect.
_____ 2. The barman gives Frederick & Catherine a ___ and food
_____ 3. He left Frederick and Piani at the farmhouse
_____ 4. Feeling of Frederick towards Catherine
_____ 5. Award
_____ 6. Rinaldi said he and Frederick were alike underneath; like ___.
_____ 7. Catherine's last name
_____ 8. A Farewell to ___
_____ 9. He was going to marry Catherine before Frederick met her.
_____ 10. They must be obeyed
_____ 11. I'm not a bit afraid. It's just a dirty ___.
_____ 12. Was shot by mistake by Italians
_____ 13. Catherine died having ___ after the operation
_____ 14. Narrator: Frederick _____
_____ 15. Dear boy, that's not ___. That is cynicism.
_____ 16. It would help keep the baby small
_____ 17. Hurt but not killed
_____ 18. Frederick Henry joined this corps
_____ 19. Frederick Henry's nationality
_____ 20. In war, one side ____s the other

A Farewell To Arms Fill In The Blanks 1 Answer Key

PRIEST	1. Rinaldi teases him, but Frederick shows some respect.
BOAT	2. The barman gives Frederick & Catherine a ___ and food
BONELLO	3. He left Frederick and Piani at the farmhouse
LOVE	4. Feeling of Frederick towards Catherine
MEDAL	5. Award
BROTHERS	6. Rinaldi said he and Frederick were alike underneath; like ___.
BARKLEY	7. Catherine's last name
ARMS	8. A Farewell to ___
RINALDI	9. He was going to marry Catherine before Frederick met her.
ORDERS	10. They must be obeyed
TRICK	11. I'm not a bit afraid. It's just a dirty ___.
AYMO	12. Was shot by mistake by Italians
HEMORRHAGES	13. Catherine died having ___ after the operation
HENRY	14. Narrator: Frederick ___
WISDOM	15. Dear boy, that's not ___. That is cynicism.
BEER	16. It would help keep the baby small
WOUNDED	17. Hurt but not killed
AMBULANCE	18. Frederick Henry joined this corps
AMERICAN	19. Frederick Henry's nationality
FIGHT	20. In war, one side ____s the other

A Farewell To Arms Fill In The Blanks 2

_____ 1. They must be obeyed

_____ 2. Catherine is afraid of it

_____ 3. It would help keep the baby small

_____ 4. The neutral country

_____ 5. Hospital supervisor; Van ____

_____ 6. Place where sick & wounded people are treated

_____ 7. Was shot by mistake by Italians

_____ 8. Author

_____ 9. Award

_____ 10. He left Frederick and Piani at the farmhouse

_____ 11. The priest brought Frederick vermouth and ___ in the hospital.

_____ 12. Catherine's profession

_____ 13. He helped Frederick and Catherine

_____ 14. A ___ person dies two thousand deaths but never mentions it

_____ 15. Friend to Frederick and Catherine

_____ 16. World ___ I

_____ 17. Name of the mountain range

_____ 18. Rinaldi said he and Frederick were alike underneath; like ___.

_____ 19. Frederick Henry's nationality

_____ 20. Catherine's condition

A Farewell To Arms Fill In The Blanks 2 Answer Key

ORDERS	1. They must be obeyed
RAIN	2. Catherine is afraid of it
BEER	3. It would help keep the baby small
SWITZERLAND	4. The neutral country
CAMPEN	5. Hospital supervisor; Van ____
HOSPITAL	6. Place where sick & wounded people are treated
AYMO	7. Was shot by mistake by Italians
HEMINGWAY	8. Author
MEDAL	9. Award
BONELLO	10. He left Frederick and Piani at the farmhouse
NEWSPAPERS	11. The priest brought Frederick vermouth and ___ in the hospital.
NURSE	12. Catherine's profession
BARMAN	13. He helped Frederick and Catherine
BRAVE	14. A ___ person dies two thousand deaths but never mentions it
GAGE	15. Friend to Frederick and Catherine
WAR	16. World ___ I
ALPS	17. Name of the mountain range
BROTHERS	18. Rinaldi said he and Frederick were alike underneath; like ___.
AMERICAN	19. Frederick Henry's nationality
PREGNANT	20. Catherine's condition

A Farewell To Arms Fill In The Blanks 3

_____ 1. Dear boy, that's not ___. That is cynicism.

_____ 2. It would help keep the baby small

_____ 3. Where Frederick was wounded

_____ 4. ___ was washed away in the river along with any obligation.

_____ 5. World ___ I

_____ 6. They must be obeyed

_____ 7. I am the ___. I am the ___ of reason.

_____ 8. Name of the mountain range

_____ 9. Rinaldi teases him, but Frederick shows some respect.

_____ 10. ___ For Me; horse they bet on

_____ 11. Author

_____ 12. Hospital supervisor; Van ____

_____ 13. Frederick Henry joined this corps

_____ 14. Friend to Frederick and Catherine

_____ 15. A ___ person dies two thousand deaths but never mentions it

_____ 16. Catherine thinks he's boring

_____ 17. The neutral country

_____ 18. Catherine's last name

_____ 19. Frederick's illness from drinking

_____ 20. Frederick played billiards with him

A Farewell To Arms Fill In The Blanks 3 Answer Key

WISDOM	1. Dear boy, that's not ___. That is cynicism.
BEER	2. It would help keep the baby small
LEG	3. Where Frederick was wounded
ANGER	4. ___ was washed away in the river along with any obligation.
WAR	5. World ___ I
ORDERS	6. They must be obeyed
SNAKE	7. I am the ___. I am the ___ of reason.
ALPS	8. Name of the mountain range
PRIEST	9. Rinaldi teases him, but Frederick shows some respect.
LIGHT	10. ___ For Me; horse they bet on
HEMINGWAY	11. Author
CAMPEN	12. Hospital supervisor; Van ___
AMBULANCE	13. Frederick Henry joined this corps
GAGE	14. Friend to Frederick and Catherine
BRAVE	15. A ___ person dies two thousand deaths but never mentions it
ETTORE	16. Catherine thinks he's boring
SWITZERLAND	17. The neutral country
BARKLEY	18. Catherine's last name
JAUNDICE	19. Frederick's illness from drinking
GREFFI	20. Frederick played billiards with him

A Farewell To Arms Fill In The Blanks 4

_____ 1. Frederick played billiards with him

_____ 2. World ___ I

_____ 3. ___ For Me; horse they bet on

_____ 4. Hospital where Catherine was transferred

_____ 5. Dear boy, that's not ___. That is cynicism.

_____ 6. He helped Frederick and Catherine

_____ 7. Place where sick & wounded people are treated

_____ 8. It would help keep the baby small

_____ 9. The neutral country

_____ 10. Name of the mountain range

_____ 11. They must be obeyed

_____ 12. A Farewell to ___

_____ 13. A true Hemingway man; fixed Frederick's knee

_____ 14. A ___ person dies two thousand deaths but never mentions it

_____ 15. Catherine's last name

_____ 16. Author

_____ 17. Award

_____ 18. Where Frederick was wounded

_____ 19. Was shot by mistake by Italians

_____ 20. Catherine's condition

A Farewell To Arms Fill In The Blanks 4 Answer Key

GREFFI	1. Frederick played billiards with him
WAR	2. World ___ I
LIGHT	3. ___ For Me; horse they bet on
MILAN	4. Hospital where Catherine was transferred
WISDOM	5. Dear boy, that's not ___. That is cynicism.
BARMAN	6. He helped Frederick and Catherine
HOSPITAL	7. Place where sick & wounded people are treated
BEER	8. It would help keep the baby small
SWITZERLAND	9. The neutral country
ALPS	10. Name of the mountain range
ORDERS	11. They must be obeyed
ARMS	12. A Farewell to ___
VALENTINI	13. A true Hemingway man; fixed Frederick's knee
BRAVE	14. A ___ person dies two thousand deaths but never mentions it
BARKLEY	15. Catherine's last name
HEMINGWAY	16. Author
MEDAL	17. Award
LEG	18. Where Frederick was wounded
AYMO	19. Was shot by mistake by Italians
PREGNANT	20. Catherine's condition

A Farewell To Arms Matching 1

___ 1. ALPS   A. A ___ To Arms
___ 2. HOSPITAL   B. Rinaldi teases him, but Frederick shows some respect.
___ 3. PEACE   C. Name of the mountain range
___ 4. LOVE   D. Place Frederick jumped into to escape
___ 5. BARMAN   E. I was going to forget the war. I had made a separate ___.
___ 6. LIFE   F. Was shot by mistake by Italians
___ 7. BEER   G. A Farewell to ___
___ 8. SNAKE   H. The priest brought Frederick vermouth and ___ in the hospital.
___ 9. FAREWELL   I. They must be obeyed
___10. BARKLEY   J. I am the ___. I am the ___ of reason.
___11. RIVER   K. Hurt but not killed
___12. ITALY   L. But ___ isn't hard to manage when you've nothing to lose.
___13. SWITZERLAND   M. Frederick's illness from drinking
___14. PRIEST   N. He helped Frederick and Catherine
___15. AMERICAN   O. Frederick Henry's nationality
___16. FIGHT   P. The neutral country
___17. AYMO   Q. The barman gives Frederick & Catherine a ___ and food
___18. NEWSPAPERS   R. Catherine's last name
___19. MILAN   S. In war, one side ___s the other
___20. WOUNDED   T. Place where story takes place
___21. BOAT   U. Hospital where Catherine was transferred
___22. ARMS   V. It would help keep the baby small
___23. JAUNDICE   W. Feeling of Frederick towards Catherine
___24. BROTHERS   X. Rinaldi said he and Frederick were alike underneath; like ___.
___25. ORDERS   Y. Place where sick & wounded people are treated

A Farewell To Arms Matching 1 Answer Key

- C - 1. ALPS
- Y - 2. HOSPITAL
- E - 3. PEACE
- W - 4. LOVE
- N - 5. BARMAN
- L - 6. LIFE
- V - 7. BEER
- J - 8. SNAKE
- A - 9. FAREWELL
- R - 10. BARKLEY
- D - 11. RIVER
- T - 12. ITALY
- P - 13. SWITZERLAND
- B - 14. PRIEST
- O - 15. AMERICAN
- S - 16. FIGHT
- F - 17. AYMO
- H - 18. NEWSPAPERS
- U - 19. MILAN
- K - 20. WOUNDED
- Q - 21. BOAT
- G - 22. ARMS
- M - 23. JAUNDICE
- X - 24. BROTHERS
- I - 25. ORDERS

A. A ___ To Arms
B. Rinaldi teases him, but Frederick shows some respect.
C. Name of the mountain range
D. Place Frederick jumped into to escape
E. I was going to forget the war. I had made a separate ___.
F. Was shot by mistake by Italians
G. A Farewell to ___
H. The priest brought Frederick vermouth and ___ in the hospital.
I. They must be obeyed
J. I am the ___. I am the ___ of reason.
K. Hurt but not killed
L. But ___ isn't hard to manage when you've nothing to lose.
M. Frederick's illness from drinking
N. He helped Frederick and Catherine
O. Frederick Henry's nationality
P. The neutral country
Q. The barman gives Frederick & Catherine a ___ and food
R. Catherine's last name
S. In war, one side ____s the other
T. Place where story takes place
U. Hospital where Catherine was transferred
V. It would help keep the baby small
W. Feeling of Frederick towards Catherine
X. Rinaldi said he and Frederick were alike underneath; like ___.
Y. Place where sick & wounded people are treated

A Farewell To Arms Matching 2

___ 1. BABY   A. Catherine gave Frederick a St. ___ medal.
___ 2. VALENTINI   B. It would help keep the baby small
___ 3. JAUNDICE   C. The barman gives Frederick & Catherine a ___ and food
___ 4. LIFE   D. A ___ person dies two thousand deaths but never mentions it
___ 5. ORDERS   E. Catherine is afraid of it
___ 6. ARMS   F. He helped Frederick and Catherine
___ 7. FAREWELL   G. Catherine thinks he's boring
___ 8. AMERICAN   H. But ___ isn't hard to manage when you've nothing to lose.
___ 9. BOAT   I. He was going to marry Catherine before Frederick met her.
___ 10. ITALY   J. A true Hemingway man; fixed Frederick's knee
___ 11. HOSPITAL   K. A Farewell to ___
___ 12. ETTORE   L. A ___ To Arms
___ 13. AYMO   M. Place where story takes place
___ 14. BRAVE   N. It was born dead
___ 15. BARMAN   O. Was shot by mistake by Italians
___ 16. HEMINGWAY   P. Frederick Henry's nationality
___ 17. PEACE   Q. They must be obeyed
___ 18. WISDOM   R. Place where sick & wounded people are treated
___ 19. RAIN   S. Name of the mountain range
___ 20. PREGNANT   T. I was going to forget the war. I had made a separate ___.
___ 21. BEER   U. Frederick's illness from drinking
___ 22. ANGER   V. Author
___ 23. RINALDI   W. Catherine's condition
___ 24. ALPS   X. ___ was washed away in the river along with any obligation.
___ 25. ANTHONY   Y. Dear boy, that's not ___. That is cynicism.

A Farewell To Arms Matching 2 Answer Key

N - 1. BABY   A. Catherine gave Frederick a St. ___ medal.
J - 2. VALENTINI   B. It would help keep the baby small
U - 3. JAUNDICE   C. The barman gives Frederick & Catherine a ___ and food
H - 4. LIFE   D. A ___ person dies two thousand deaths but never mentions it
Q - 5. ORDERS   E. Catherine is afraid of it
K - 6. ARMS   F. He helped Frederick and Catherine
L - 7. FAREWELL   G. Catherine thinks he's boring
P - 8. AMERICAN   H. But ___ isn't hard to manage when you've nothing to lose.
C - 9. BOAT   I. He was going to marry Catherine before Frederick met her.
M -10. ITALY   J. A true Hemingway man; fixed Frederick's knee
R -11. HOSPITAL   K. A Farewell to ___
G -12. ETTORE   L. A ___ To Arms
O -13. AYMO   M. Place where story takes place
D -14. BRAVE   N. It was born dead
F -15. BARMAN   O. Was shot by mistake by Italians
V -16. HEMINGWAY   P. Frederick Henry's nationality
T -17. PEACE   Q. They must be obeyed
Y -18. WISDOM   R. Place where sick & wounded people are treated
E -19. RAIN   S. Name of the mountain range
W -20. PREGNANT   T. I was going to forget the war. I had made a separate ___.
B -21. BEER   U. Frederick's illness from drinking
X -22. ANGER   V. Author
I - 23. RINALDI   W. Catherine's condition
S -24. ALPS   X. ___ was washed away in the river along with any obligation.
A -25. ANTHONY   Y. Dear boy, that's not ___. That is cynicism.

A Farewell To Arms Matching 3

___ 1. FAREWELL   A. A Farewell to ___
___ 2. ETTORE   B. Rinaldi teases him, but Frederick shows some respect.
___ 3. LIFE   C. Was shot by mistake by Italians
___ 4. SNAKE   D. Feeling of Frederick towards Catherine
___ 5. ITALY   E. Narrator: Frederick _____
___ 6. WAR   F. Hospital supervisor; Van ____
___ 7. BEER   G. ___ was washed away in the river along with any obligation.
___ 8. SWITZERLAND   H. Place Frederick jumped into to escape
___ 9. VALENTINI   I. Catherine's last name
___10. LEG   J. Dear boy, that's not ___. That is cynicism.
___11. ARMS   K. ___ For Me; horse they bet on
___12. PRIEST   L. Place where story takes place
___13. RINALDI   M. The neutral country
___14. CAMPEN   N. Where Frederick was wounded
___15. LOVE   O. Catherine's profession
___16. BONELLO   P. He was going to marry Catherine before Frederick met her.
___17. WISDOM   Q. Catherine thinks he's boring
___18. BARKLEY   R. Frederick played billiards with him
___19. AYMO   S. He left Frederick and Piani at the farmhouse
___20. HENRY   T. A true Hemingway man; fixed Frederick's knee
___21. NURSE   U. It would help keep the baby small
___22. GREFFI   V. World ___ I
___23. ANGER   W. But ___ isn't hard to manage when you've nothing to lose.
___24. LIGHT   X. I am the ___. I am the ___ of reason.
___25. RIVER   Y. A ___ To Arms

A Farewell To Arms Matching 3 Answer Key

Y - 1.	FAREWELL	A.	A Farewell to ___
Q - 2.	ETTORE	B.	Rinaldi teases him, but Frederick shows some respect.
W - 3.	LIFE	C.	Was shot by mistake by Italians
X - 4.	SNAKE	D.	Feeling of Frederick towards Catherine
L - 5.	ITALY	E.	Narrator: Frederick _____
V - 6.	WAR	F.	Hospital supervisor; Van ____
U - 7.	BEER	G.	___ was washed away in the river along with any obligation.
M - 8.	SWITZERLAND	H.	Place Frederick jumped into to escape
T - 9.	VALENTINI	I.	Catherine's last name
N - 10.	LEG	J.	Dear boy, that's not ___. That is cynicism.
A - 11.	ARMS	K.	___ For Me; horse they bet on
B - 12.	PRIEST	L.	Place where story takes place
P - 13.	RINALDI	M.	The neutral country
F - 14.	CAMPEN	N.	Where Frederick was wounded
D - 15.	LOVE	O.	Catherine's profession
S - 16.	BONELLO	P.	He was going to marry Catherine before Frederick met her.
J - 17.	WISDOM	Q.	Catherine thinks he's boring
I - 18.	BARKLEY	R.	Frederick played billiards with him
C - 19.	AYMO	S.	He left Frederick and Piani at the farmhouse
E - 20.	HENRY	T.	A true Hemingway man; fixed Frederick's knee
O - 21.	NURSE	U.	It would help keep the baby small
R - 22.	GREFFI	V.	World ___ I
G - 23.	ANGER	W.	But ___ isn't hard to manage when you've nothing to lose.
K - 24.	LIGHT	X.	I am the ___. I am the ___ of reason.
H - 25.	RIVER	Y.	A ___ To Arms

A Farewell To Arms Matching 4

___ 1. BARMAN   A. The priest brought Frederick vermouth and ___ in the hospital.
___ 2. HOSPITAL   B. A Farewell to ___
___ 3. NEWSPAPERS   C. Catherine thinks he's boring
___ 4. PEACE   D. He helped Frederick and Catherine
___ 5. ITALY   E. World ___ I
___ 6. SWITZERLAND   F. Place where sick & wounded people are treated
___ 7. AYMO   G. Frederick Henry's nationality
___ 8. FIGHT   H. Author
___ 9. PRIEST   I. Place where story takes place
___10. ANTHONY   J. Catherine gave Frederick a St. ___ medal.
___11. WAR   K. Narrator: Frederick ___
___12. AMBULANCE   L. It was born dead
___13. JAUNDICE   M. Frederick Henry joined this corps
___14. RINALDI   N. Frederick's illness from drinking
___15. ETTORE   O. Dear boy, that's not ___. That is cynicism.
___16. WISDOM   P. In war, one side ___s the other
___17. BROTHERS   Q. Feeling of Frederick towards Catherine
___18. FAREWELL   R. A ___ To Arms
___19. HENRY   S. Was shot by mistake by Italians
___20. LOVE   T. I am the ___. I am the ___ of reason.
___21. AMERICAN   U. Rinaldi teases him, but Frederick shows some respect.
___22. HEMINGWAY   V. I was going to forget the war. I had made a separate ___.
___23. BABY   W. The neutral country
___24. SNAKE   X. He was going to marry Catherine before Frederick met her.
___25. ARMS   Y. Rinaldi said he and Frederick were alike underneath; like ___.

A Farewell To Arms Matching 4 Answer Key

D - 1. BARMAN   A. The priest brought Frederick vermouth and ___ in the hospital.
F - 2. HOSPITAL   B. A Farewell to ___
A - 3. NEWSPAPERS   C. Catherine thinks he's boring
V - 4. PEACE   D. He helped Frederick and Catherine
I - 5. ITALY   E. World ___ I
W - 6. SWITZERLAND   F. Place where sick & wounded people are treated
S - 7. AYMO   G. Frederick Henry's nationality
P - 8. FIGHT   H. Author
U - 9. PRIEST   I. Place where story takes place
J - 10. ANTHONY   J. Catherine gave Frederick a St. ___ medal.
E - 11. WAR   K. Narrator: Frederick _____
M - 12. AMBULANCE   L. It was born dead
N - 13. JAUNDICE   M. Frederick Henry joined this corps
X - 14. RINALDI   N. Frederick's illness from drinking
C - 15. ETTORE   O. Dear boy, that's not ___. That is cynicism.
O - 16. WISDOM   P. In war, one side ___s the other
Y - 17. BROTHERS   Q. Feeling of Frederick towards Catherine
R - 18. FAREWELL   R. A ___ To Arms
K - 19. HENRY   S. Was shot by mistake by Italians
Q - 20. LOVE   T. I am the ___. I am the ___ of reason.
G - 21. AMERICAN   U. Rinaldi teases him, but Frederick shows some respect.
H - 22. HEMINGWAY   V. I was going to forget the war. I had made a separate ___.
L - 23. BABY   W. The neutral country
T - 24. SNAKE   X. He was going to marry Catherine before Frederick met her.
B - 25. ARMS   Y. Rinaldi said he and Frederick were alike underneath; like ___.

A Farewell To Arms Magic Squares 1

A. BONELLO E. HENRY   I. PEACE   M. ANGER
B. BEER   F. ITALY   J. ALPS   N. GREFFI
C. BABY   G. PREGNANT   K. RAIN   O. FAREWELL
D. WISDOM   H. AMBULANCE L. HEMORRHAGES   P. LIFE

1. He left Frederick and Piani at the farmhouse
2. Frederick played billiards with him
3. Name of the mountain range
4. Narrator: Frederick _____
5. Catherine's condition
6. Catherine died having ___ after the operation
7. But ___ isn't hard to manage when you've nothing to lose.
8. It was born dead
9. A ___ To Arms
10. Dear boy, that's not ___. That is cynicism.
11. Frederick Henry joined this corps
12. Catherine is afraid of it
13. I was going to forget the war. I had made a separate ___.
14. Place where story takes place
15. It would help keep the baby small
16. ___ was washed away in the river along with any obligation.

A=	B=	C=	D=
E=	F=	G=	H=
I=	J=	K=	L=
M=	N=	O=	P=

A Farewell To Arms Magic Squares 1 Answer Key

A. BONELLO   E. HENRY   I. PEACE   M. ANGER
B. BEER   F. ITALY   J. ALPS   N. GREFFI
C. BABY   G. PREGNANT   K. RAIN   O. FAREWELL
D. WISDOM   H. AMBULANCE L. HEMORRHAGES   P. LIFE

1. He left Frederick and Piani at the farmhouse
2. Frederick played billiards with him
3. Name of the mountain range
4. Narrator: Frederick _____
5. Catherine's condition
6. Catherine died having ___ after the operation
7. But ___ isn't hard to manage when you've nothing to lose.
8. It was born dead
9. A ___ To Arms
10. Dear boy, that's not ___. That is cynicism.
11. Frederick Henry joined this corps
12. Catherine is afraid of it
13. I was going to forget the war. I had made a separate ___.
14. Place where story takes place
15. It would help keep the baby small
16. ___ was washed away in the river along with any obligation.

A=1	B=15	C=8	D=10
E=4	F=14	G=5	H=11
I=13	J=3	K=12	L=6
M=16	N=2	O=9	P=7

A Farewell To Arms Magic Squares 2

A. WOUNDED E. LIGHT I. RAIN M. VALENTINI
B. BEER F. LOVE J. NURSE N. CAMPEN
C. AMERICAN G. WISDOM K. SNAKE O. ANTHONY
D. HEMORRHAGES H. JAUNDICE L. FAREWELL P. BABY

1. It would help keep the baby small
2. Dear boy, that's not ___. That is cynicism.
3. I am the ___. I am the ___ of reason.
4. Hospital supervisor; Van ____
5. A true Hemingway man; fixed Frederick's knee
6. A ___ To Arms
7. Frederick's illness from drinking
8. Hurt but not killed
9. It was born dead
10. Catherine is afraid of it
11. ___ For Me; horse they bet on
12. Catherine died having ___ after the operation
13. Frederick Henry's nationality
14. Feeling of Frederick towards Catherine
15. Catherine's profession
16. Catherine gave Frederick a St. ___ medal.

A=	B=	C=	D=
E=	F=	G=	H=
I=	J=	K=	L=
M=	N=	O=	P=

A Farewell To Arms Magic Squares 2 Answer Key

A. WOUNDED
B. BEER
C. AMERICAN
D. HEMORRHAGES

E. LIGHT
F. LOVE
G. WISDOM
H. JAUNDICE

I. RAIN
J. NURSE
K. SNAKE
L. FAREWELL

M. VALENTINI
N. CAMPEN
O. ANTHONY
P. BABY

1. It would help keep the baby small
2. Dear boy, that's not ___. That is cynicism.
3. I am the ___. I am the ___ of reason.
4. Hospital supervisor; Van ____
5. A true Hemingway man; fixed Frederick's knee
6. A ___ To Arms
7. Frederick's illness from drinking
8. Hurt but not killed
9. It was born dead
10. Catherine is afraid of it
11. ___ For Me; horse they bet on
12. Catherine died having ___ after the operation
13. Frederick Henry's nationality
14. Feeling of Frederick towards Catherine
15. Catherine's profession
16. Catherine gave Frederick a St. ___ medal.

A=8	B=1	C=13	D=12
E=11	F=14	G=2	H=7
I=10	J=15	K=3	L=6
M=5	N=4	O=16	P=9

A Farewell To Arms Magic Squares 3

A. BROTHERS
B. NURSE
C. BEER
D. AMBULANCE
E. PRIEST
F. CAMPEN
G. AMERICAN
H. GAGE
I. GREFFI
J. BONELLO
K. ALPS
L. NEWSPAPERS
M. PREGNANT
N. TRICK
O. VALENTINI
P. BARMAN

1. Catherine's condition
2. Hospital supervisor; Van ____
3. Friend to Frederick and Catherine
4. A true Hemingway man; fixed Frederick's knee
5. The priest brought Frederick vermouth and ___ in the hospital.
6. It would help keep the baby small
7. Rinaldi said he and Frederick were alike underneath; like ___.
8. He left Frederick and Piani at the farmhouse
9. Name of the mountain range
10. Frederick Henry joined this corps
11. Catherine's profession
12. Frederick played billiards with him
13. I'm not a bit afraid. It's just a dirty
14. Rinaldi teases him, but Frederick shows some respect.
15. Frederick Henry's nationality
16. He helped Frederick and Catherine

A=	B=	C=	D=
E=	F=	G=	H=
I=	J=	K=	L=
M=	N=	O=	P=

A Farewell To Arms Magic Squares 3 Answer Key

A. BROTHERS   E. PRIEST   I. GREFFI   M. PREGNANT
B. NURSE   F. CAMPEN   J. BONELLO   N. TRICK
C. BEER   G. AMERICAN K. ALPS   O. VALENTINI
D. AMBULANCE H. GAGE   L. NEWSPAPERS   P. BARMAN

1. Catherine's condition
2. Hospital supervisor; Van ____
3. Friend to Frederick and Catherine
4. A true Hemingway man; fixed Frederick's knee
5. The priest brought Frederick vermouth and ___ in the hospital.
6. It would help keep the baby small
7. Rinaldi said he and Frederick were alike underneath; like ___.
8. He left Frederick and Piani at the farmhouse
9. Name of the mountain range
10. Frederick Henry joined this corps
11. Catherine's profession
12. Frederick played billiards with him
13. I'm not a bit afraid. It's just a dirty
14. Rinaldi teases him, but Frederick shows some respect.
15. Frederick Henry's nationality
16. He helped Frederick and Catherine

A=7	B=11	C=6	D=10
E=14	F=2	G=15	H=3
I=12	J=8	K=9	L=5
M=1	N=13	O=4	P=16

A Farewell To Arms Magic Squares 4

A. ANTHONY   E. LIGHT   I. ALPS   M. FIGHT
B. AMERICAN   F. TRICK   J. WOUNDED   N. AMBULANCE
C. FAREWELL   G. BARMAN   K. BARKLEY   O. GAGE
D. NEWSPAPERS   H. HEMORRHAGES   L. HENRY   P. VALENTINI

1. Catherine died having ___ after the operation
2. Catherine gave Frederick a St. ___ medal.
3. Frederick Henry's nationality
4. He helped Frederick and Catherine
5. Hurt but not killed
6. Friend to Frederick and Catherine
7. A true Hemingway man; fixed Frederick's knee
8. Name of the mountain range
9. Catherine's last name
10. Frederick Henry joined this corps
11. In war, one side ___s the other
12. Narrator: Frederick ___
13. ___ For Me; horse they bet on
14. The priest brought Frederick vermouth and ___ in the hospital.
15. A ___ To Arms
16. I'm not a bit afraid. It's just a dirty

A=	B=	C=	D=
E=	F=	G=	H=
I=	J=	K=	L=
M=	N=	O=	P=

A Farewell To Arms Magic Squares 4 Answer Key

A. ANTHONY   E. LIGHT   I. ALPS   M. FIGHT
B. AMERICAN   F. TRICK   J. WOUNDED   N. AMBULANCE
C. FAREWELL   G. BARMAN   K. BARKLEY   O. GAGE
D. NEWSPAPERS H. HEMORRHAGES   L. HENRY   P. VALENTINI

1. Catherine died having ___ after the operation
2. Catherine gave Frederick a St. ___ medal.
3. Frederick Henry's nationality
4. He helped Frederick and Catherine
5. Hurt but not killed
6. Friend to Frederick and Catherine
7. A true Hemingway man; fixed Frederick's knee
8. Name of the mountain range
9. Catherine's last name
10. Frederick Henry joined this corps
11. In war, one side ____s the other
12. Narrator: Frederick _____
13. ___ For Me; horse they bet on
14. The priest brought Frederick vermouth and ___ in the hospital.
15. A ___ To Arms
16. I'm not a bit afraid. It's just a dirty

A=2	B=3	C=15	D=14
E=13	F=16	G=4	H=1
I=8	J=5	K=9	L=12
M=11	N=10	O=6	P=7

A Farewell To Arms Word Search 1

```
W S H S S W I T Z E R L A N D F I G H T
O X C N D N J T Q L I G H T T L T E C D
U R C F N G A B S N S J E C I D N U A J
N M D D G Q Y K R M L L E W E R A F B J
D T S E I R P Y E A I T A L Y L N Y R N
E V P R R R N T P L M K W N J D G A O D
D X W Z I S R S A T K E B I F Y E W T N
V C B V T B M S P P T R R V S L R G H K
T Z E P Z X O X S S G V A I O D P N E W
B R E S V C D N W R N P V V C C O I R K
N U R S E L I F E G A G E V K A R M S L
X B B I B K G C N L P E A A L M N E B M
W L O Y N A N T Y L L Q P C P A H A V
A Y A H K A B K A V E O S N E E N G R V
R T T C L F L Y B N A L I M T N T R M R
T G I U H Q T D T I G S Y E T K H E A N
F R B C D C Z I I A T E V D O H O F N G
T M A Y M O N K Y R N S R A R T N F J D
A K T R Q I B A R K L E Y L E X Y I P P
```

A Farewell to ___ (4)
A ___ To Arms (8)
A ___ person dies two thousand deaths but never mentions it (5)
A true Hemingway man; fixed Frederick's knee (9)
Author (9)
Award (5)
But ___ isn't hard to manage when you've nothing to lose. (4)
Catherine gave Frederick a St. ___ medal. (7)
Catherine is afraid of it (4)
Catherine thinks he's boring (6)
Catherine's condition (8)
Catherine's last name (7)
Catherine's profession (5)
Dear boy, that's not ___. That is cynicism. (6)
Feeling of Frederick towards Catherine (4)
Frederick Henry joined this corps (9)
Frederick Henry's nationality (8)
Frederick played billiards with him (6)
Frederick's illness from drinking (8)
Friend to Frederick and Catherine (4)
He helped Frederick and Catherine (6)
He left Frederick and Piani at the farmhouse (7)
He was going to marry Catherine before Frederick met her. (7)
Hospital supervisor; Van ___ (6)
Hospital where Catherine was transferred (5)

Hurt but not killed (7)
I am the ___. I am the ___ of reason. (5)
I was going to forget the war. I had made a separate ___. (5)
I'm not a bit afraid. It's just a dirty ___. (5)
In war, one side ___s the other (5)
It was born dead (4)
It would help keep the baby small (4)
Name of the mountain range (4)
Narrator: Frederick _____ (5)
Place Frederick jumped into to escape (5)
Place where story takes place (5)
Rinaldi said he and Frederick were alike underneath; like ___. (8)
Rinaldi teases him, but Frederick shows some respect. (6)
The barman gives Frederick & Catherine a ___ and food (4)
The neutral country (11)
The priest brought Frederick vermouth and ___ in the hospital. (10)
They must be obeyed (6)
Was shot by mistake by Italians (4)
Where Frederick was wounded (3)
World ___ I (3)
___ For Me; horse they bet on (5)
___ was washed away in the river along with any obligation. (5)

A Farewell To Arms Word Search 1 Answer Key

```
W              S   I   T   Z   E   R   L   A   N   D   F   I   G   H   T
O                  N           L       G   H   T           T       E
U       R              A           S           E   C   I   D   N   U   A   J
N       D                  K   R       L   L   E   W   E   R   A   F       B
D   T   S   E   I   R   P       E       I   T   A   L   Y       N   Y       R
E           R   R               P       M       W               G   A       O
D           I   S               A           E   B   I               E   W   T
        B   V       B           P           R       S   L       R   G   H
        E           O           S           A   I   O   D   P   N       E
    R   E               N   W           P   V   V   C   C   O       I       R
N   U   R   S   E   L   I   F   E   G   A   G   E   V       A   R   M   S
        B       I   B           C   N   L       E   A   A   L   M   N   E   B
W       O       N       N               L   L   P   C   P   A       H   A
A       A   K   B           A           E   O   S       E   E   N   G   A
R       T   C   L       L   Y       N   A   L   I   M   T   N   T   R   M
        I   U                       D   T   I   G           E   T       H   E
        R   B                           I   I   A           D   O       O   F   N
T       M   A   Y   M   O   N               R           R   A   R       N   F
A                   I   B   A   R   K   L   E   Y       L       E       Y   I
```

A Farewell to ___ (4)
A ___ To Arms (8)
A ___ person dies two thousand deaths but never mentions it (5)
A true Hemingway man; fixed Frederick's knee (9)
Author (9)
Award (5)
But ___ isn't hard to manage when you've nothing to lose. (4)
Catherine gave Frederick a St. ___ medal. (7)
Catherine is afraid of it (4)
Catherine thinks he's boring (6)
Catherine's condition (8)
Catherine's last name (7)
Catherine's profession (5)
Dear boy, that's not ___. That is cynicism. (6)
Feeling of Frederick towards Catherine (4)
Frederick Henry joined this corps (9)
Frederick Henry's nationality (8)
Frederick played billiards with him (6)
Frederick's illness from drinking (8)
Friend to Frederick and Catherine (4)
He helped Frederick and Catherine (6)
He left Frederick and Piani at the farmhouse (7)
He was going to marry Catherine before Frederick met her. (7)
Hospital supervisor; Van ___ (6)
Hospital where Catherine was transferred (5)
Hurt but not killed (7)
I am the ___. I am the ___ of reason. (5)
I was going to forget the war. I had made a separate ___. (5)
I'm not a bit afraid. It's just a dirty ___. (5)
In war, one side ___s the other (5)
It was born dead (4)
It would help keep the baby small (4)
Name of the mountain range (4)
Narrator: Frederick _____ (5)
Place Frederick jumped into to escape (5)
Place where story takes place (5)
Rinaldi said he and Frederick were alike underneath; like ___. (8)
Rinaldi teases him, but Frederick shows some respect. (6)
The barman gives Frederick & Catherine a ___ and food (4)
The neutral country (11)
The priest brought Frederick vermouth and ___ in the hospital. (10)
They must be obeyed (6)
Was shot by mistake by Italians (4)
Where Frederick was wounded (3)
World ___ I (3)
___ For Me; horse they bet on (5)
___ was washed away in the river along with any obligation. (5)

A Farewell To Arms Word Search 2

```
W O U N D E D P L H M C R A B B H V H S
F J D B O N E L L O M I L A N R T A O R
C J B V K C X W D R V P A J J A N L S S
B Q A F L R A S Y E S E D H O V A E P T
T T B U J A I N R N L N E B V E N N I R
R C Y A N W Z A G C Y I M S V B G T T V
I S O M E D R Q A E Q A G C B A E I A T
C P R B W M I L G P R R C H N R R N L Z
K E D U S H D C E X R E E B T K P I E X
P A E L P E H A E L L I R X S L J D R Q
K C R A A N K M C E A O E L T E P L O V
K E S N P R B P W G T M L S C Y L A T I
F J S C E Y C E L H R A E I T X T N T T
P V B E R T G N E R W E N R F M S U E N
T V B A S R E R G Y T M F T I E M R V X
A Y M O R K S G G H W W Z F H C K S G Z
C J S S A M J K G P F R K K I O A E F B
V Y Y N D C A I D L A N I R R D N N X Z
T R S Z W M F N F A R E W E L L P Y X D
```

A Farewell to ___ (4)
A ___ To Arms (8)
A ___ person dies two thousand deaths but never mentions it (5)
A true Hemingway man; fixed Frederick's knee (9)
Award (5)
But ___ isn't hard to manage when you've nothing to lose. (4)
Catherine gave Frederick a St. ___ medal. (7)
Catherine is afraid of it (4)
Catherine thinks he's boring (6)
Catherine's condition (8)
Catherine's last name (7)
Catherine's profession (5)
Dear boy, that's not ___. That is cynicism. (6)
Feeling of Frederick towards Catherine (4)
Frederick Henry joined this corps (9)
Frederick Henry's nationality (8)
Frederick played billiards with him (6)
Frederick's illness from drinking (8)
Friend to Frederick and Catherine (4)
He helped Frederick and Catherine (6)
He left Frederick and Piani at the farmhouse (7)
He was going to marry Catherine before Frederick met her. (7)
Hospital supervisor; Van ____ (6)
Hospital where Catherine was transferred (5)
Hurt but not killed (7)

I am the ___. I am the ___ of reason. (5)
I was going to forget the war. I had made a separate ___. (5)
I'm not a bit afraid. It's just a dirty ___. (5)
In war, one side ___s the other (5)
It was born dead (4)
It would help keep the baby small (4)
Name of the mountain range (4)
Narrator: Frederick _____ (5)
Place Frederick jumped into to escape (5)
Place where sick & wounded people are treated (8)
Place where story takes place (5)
Rinaldi said he and Frederick were alike underneath; like ___. (8)
Rinaldi teases him, but Frederick shows some respect. (6)
The barman gives Frederick & Catherine a ___ and food (4)
The priest brought Frederick vermouth and ___ in the hospital. (10)
They must be obeyed (6)
Was shot by mistake by Italians (4)
Where Frederick was wounded (3)
World ___ I (3)
___ For Me; horse they bet on (5)
___ was washed away in the river along with any obligation. (5)

A Farewell To Arms Word Search 2 Answer Key

```
W O U N D E D     L     M   R A     B   V H
      B O N E L L O M I L A N   R T A O
    J B           D   V P A     A N L S
    A     R A S E S E D   O V A E P
T   B U A I N R     L N E B   E N N I
R   Y A N W   A G       I M   B G T T
I   O M E D R   A E     A G   A E I A
C P R B W M I   G P R   R H   R R N L
K E D U S H   C E R E E B T K P I E
  A E L P E   A E L I R     L     R
  C R A A N   M E A O E     E     O
  E S N P R   P G T M L S   Y L A T I
      C E Y   E H R A E I T       N T
      B   R   N E   N R F         U E
          A S     E   T F T I     R
  A Y M O R K S     H     F H C   S
              A M       G     I O A E
            N       A I D L A N I R N N
          S       F N F A R E W E L L   Y
```

A Farewell to ___ (4)
A ___ To Arms (8)
A ___ person dies two thousand deaths but never mentions it (5)
A true Hemingway man; fixed Frederick's knee (9)
Award (5)
But ___ isn't hard to manage when you've nothing to lose. (4)
Catherine gave Frederick a St. ___ medal. (7)
Catherine is afraid of it (4)
Catherine thinks he's boring (6)
Catherine's condition (8)
Catherine's last name (7)
Catherine's profession (5)
Dear boy, that's not ___. That is cynicism. (6)
Feeling of Frederick towards Catherine (4)
Frederick Henry joined this corps (9)
Frederick Henry's nationality (8)
Frederick played billiards with him (6)
Frederick's illness from drinking (8)
Friend to Frederick and Catherine (4)
He helped Frederick and Catherine (6)
He left Frederick and Piani at the farmhouse (7)
He was going to marry Catherine before Frederick met her. (7)
Hospital supervisor; Van ___ (6)
Hospital where Catherine was transferred (5)
Hurt but not killed (7)

I am the ___. I am the ___ of reason. (5)
I was going to forget the war. I had made a separate ___. (5)
I'm not a bit afraid. It's just a dirty ___. (5)
In war, one side ___s the other (5)
It was born dead (4)
It would help keep the baby small (4)
Name of the mountain range (4)
Narrator: Frederick _____ (5)
Place Frederick jumped into to escape (5)
Place where sick & wounded people are treated (8)
Place where story takes place (5)
Rinaldi said he and Frederick were alike underneath; like ___. (8)
Rinaldi teases him, but Frederick shows some respect. (6)
The barman gives Frederick & Catherine a ___ and food (4)
The priest brought Frederick vermouth and ___ in the hospital. (10)
They must be obeyed (6)
Was shot by mistake by Italians (4)
Where Frederick was wounded (3)
World ___ I (3)
___ For Me; horse they bet on (5)
___ was washed away in the river along with any obligation. (5)

A Farewell To Arms Word Search 3

```
B O N E L L O H F O B M F A R E W E L L
G A F R I K R O I R E Y I B N S R D Q V
P I R G L B T S G D E W P L K T Z E K C
L C H K K G J P H E R E I X A R H V N P
T T G E L C K I T R A R M S J N A O D V
R T C T W E Y T J S B O N L D M J L N S
I B N Z A G Y A A K G T Y Z B O Z W A Y
C R X W M Z T L U C J T F U B Q M O L L
K O P R E G N A N T W E L Q E M B U R G
W T E D R G X Q D P V A L Y S M Q N E J
W H A C I T A M I B N C T Y R E D D Z V
H E C L C C H G C C D Y L Q U D G E T X
S R E P A P S W E N W A R I N A L D I Z
D S N B N R J H H H T W Y P M L N J W X
C L R O Y I Z M Y I E G M M T F B G S P
A S N A K E B A R M A N Y K O G R B E G
M L B T W S V D H M I I R G J E A A J R
P P P W H T J V R A C M L Y F D V B H T
E T Y S Z P Z M R X P E V F C Q E Y P G
N V A L E N T I N I H H I R I V E R C Q
```

ALPS	BEER	GREFFI	MEDAL	RIVER
AMBULANCE	BOAT	HEMINGWAY	MILAN	SNAKE
AMERICAN	BONELLO	HENRY	NEWSPAPERS	SWITZERLAND
ANGER	BRAVE	HOSPITAL	NURSE	TRICK
ANTHONY	BROTHERS	ITALY	ORDERS	VALENTINI
ARMS	CAMPEN	JAUNDICE	PEACE	WAR
AYMO	ETTORE	LEG	PREGNANT	WISDOM
BABY	FAREWELL	LIFE	PRIEST	WOUNDED
BARKLEY	FIGHT	LIGHT	RAIN	
BARMAN	GAGE	LOVE	RINALDI	

A Farewell To Arms Word Search 3 Answer Key

```
B O N E L L O H   F   O   B   M F A R E W E L L
  A F I       O   I       I   I   N     T     E
  I R G       S   G   D   W   L       T     V
L T H K       P   H   E   E       S   H   H   O
T T G E L     I   T   R   A R M S   N   A   O D
R         E   T   J   S       D M   N D   N
I   B     A   A   A           B     O   W   A
C   R     M   L   U       T   U         O   L Y
K   O P R E G N A N T     E       S M   U   R
    T   E   R           A       R E     N   E
    H   I   G       N   N   Y   U D     D   Z
    E   C   A   G C     W   L   D       E   T
S   R E P A P S W E N   A R I N A L D   I   W
    S   B   N   R       H   W   L   N     G   W
C           O   I       I   Y   M       B   S E
A   S N A K E B A R M A N   R       E   A       R
M   L       T   S         I   Y F   V   B
P       P       T       A   M   F   E   Y
E                       R   E       R
N V A L E N T I N I     H I R I V E R
```

ALPS	BEER	GREFFI	MEDAL	RIVER
AMBULANCE	BOAT	HEMINGWAY	MILAN	SNAKE
AMERICAN	BONELLO	HENRY	NEWSPAPERS	SWITZERLAND
ANGER	BRAVE	HOSPITAL	NURSE	TRICK
ANTHONY	BROTHERS	ITALY	ORDERS	VALENTINI
ARMS	CAMPEN	JAUNDICE	PEACE	WAR
AYMO	ETTORE	LEG	PREGNANT	WISDOM
BABY	FAREWELL	LIFE	PRIEST	WOUNDED
BARKLEY	FIGHT	LIGHT	RAIN	
BARMAN	GAGE	LOVE	RINALDI	

A Farewell To Arms Word Search 4

```
A Y M O W T N G B R A V E V Q Z L V A C
J M F I A V Q R D A J V M A D O I J L M
N L E O L R F E Z W B A Y L V J F C P S
B T B R K A W F L Y S Y U E Y F E S S N
Y L A T I C N F P E A C E N S N A K E Z
Q H B N F C P I S S Z F W T D F Q P W G
J X S L M F A R E W E L L I S I M T Y X
B J E B T J C N E N F D D N S A C T P R
S A S L H S C C A Q K L B I C D Y E P T
M P R T G X N K N D A B E Y S N O R F H
Q K U K I A Q H G D Y M E M O Y E M I R
R I N A L D I H E M O R R H A G E S G S
L Y B U N E P M R M Y A T I N E Z A H C
Z Q B W T W Y R B P I N H A V L G B T F
W M Z T Y N Z M O R A N N E O E A F T R
A W O U N D E D N I A T G K N R R A D
J R Q C R Q L H E E C I C W M R D W J H
E Z R W J Q Y Q L S D I N A A C Y E R T
H O S P I T A L L T R X N T M Y R X R C
B R O T H E R S O T N E W S P A P E R S
```

ALPS	BEER	GREFFI	LOVE	RINALDI
AMBULANCE	BOAT	HEMINGWAY	MEDAL	RIVER
AMERICAN	BONELLO	HEMORRHAGES	MILAN	SNAKE
ANGER	BRAVE	HENRY	NEWSPAPERS	TRICK
ANTHONY	BROTHERS	HOSPITAL	NURSE	VALENTINI
ARMS	CAMPEN	ITALY	ORDERS	WAR
AYMO	ETTORE	JAUNDICE	PEACE	WISDOM
BABY	FAREWELL	LEG	PREGNANT	WOUNDED
BARKLEY	FIGHT	LIFE	PRIEST	
BARMAN	GAGE	LIGHT	RAIN	

A Farewell To Arms Word Search 4 Answer Key

ALPS	BEER	GREFFI	LOVE	RINALDI
AMBULANCE	BOAT	HEMINGWAY	MEDAL	RIVER
AMERICAN	BONELLO	HEMORRHAGES	MILAN	SNAKE
ANGER	BRAVE	HENRY	NEWSPAPERS	TRICK
ANTHONY	BROTHERS	HOSPITAL	NURSE	VALENTINI
ARMS	CAMPEN	ITALY	ORDERS	WAR
AYMO	ETTORE	JAUNDICE	PEACE	WISDOM
BABY	FAREWELL	LEG	PREGNANT	WOUNDED
BARKLEY	FIGHT	LIFE	PRIEST	
BARMAN	GAGE	LIGHT	RAIN	

A Farewell To Arms Crossword 1

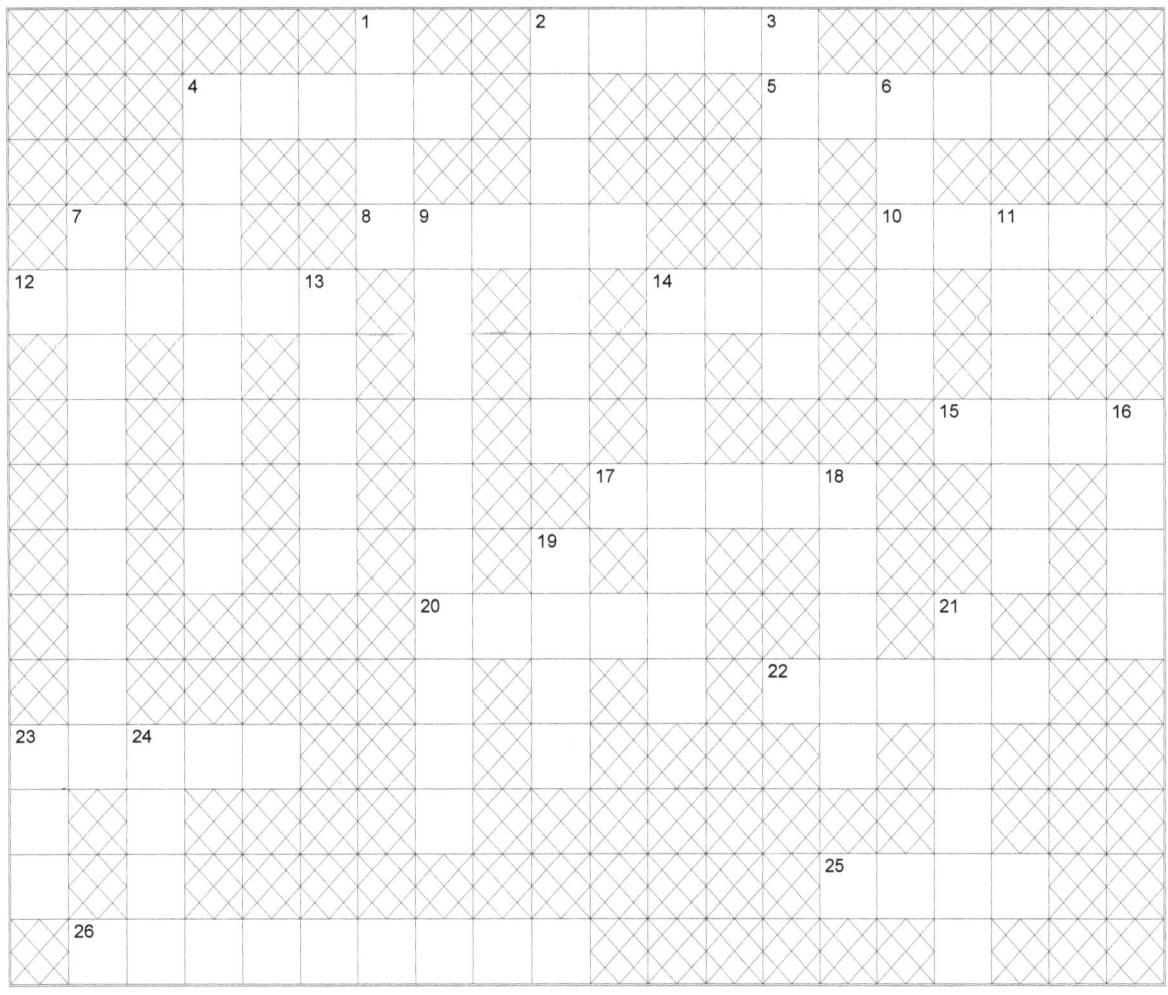

Across
2. A ___ person dies two thousand deaths but never mentions it
4. Narrator: Frederick ___
5. I'm not a bit afraid. It's just a dirty ___.
8. I am the ___. I am the ___ of reason.
10. Name of the mountain range
12. Hospital supervisor; Van ___
14. World ___ I
15. It would help keep the baby small
17. ___ was washed away in the river along with any obligation.
20. I was going to forget the war. I had made a separate ___.
22. Award
23. ___ For Me; horse they bet on
25. The barman gives Frederick & Catherine a ___ and food
26. Author

Down
1. A Farewell to ___
2. Catherine's last name
3. Catherine thinks he's boring
4. Place where sick & wounded people are treated
6. Place where story takes place
7. A true Hemingway man; fixed Frederick's knee
9. The priest brought Frederick vermouth and ___ in the hospital.
11. Rinaldi teases him, but Frederick shows some respect.
13. Catherine's profession
14. Hurt but not killed
16. Catherine is afraid of it
18. Place Frederick jumped into to escape
19. It was born dead
21. He helped Frederick and Catherine
23. Where Frederick was wounded
24. Friend to Frederick and Catherine

A Farewell To Arms Crossword 1 Answer Key

Across
2. A ___ person dies two thousand deaths but never mentions it
4. Narrator: Frederick _____
5. I'm not a bit afraid. It's just a dirty ___.
8. I am the ___. I am the ___ of reason.
10. Name of the mountain range
12. Hospital supervisor; Van ____
14. World ___ I
15. It would help keep the baby small
17. ___ was washed away in the river along with any obligation.
20. I was going to forget the war. I had made a separate ___.
22. Award
23. ___ For Me; horse they bet on
25. The barman gives Frederick & Catherine a ___ and food
26. Author

Down
1. A Farewell to ___
2. Catherine's last name
3. Catherine thinks he's boring
4. Place where sick & wounded people are treated
6. Place where story takes place
7. A true Hemingway man; fixed Frederick's knee
9. The priest brought Frederick vermouth and ___ in the hospital.
11. Rinaldi teases him, but Frederick shows some respect.
13. Catherine's profession
14. Hurt but not killed
16. Catherine is afraid of it
18. Place Frederick jumped into to escape
19. It was born dead
21. He helped Frederick and Catherine
23. Where Frederick was wounded
24. Friend to Frederick and Catherine

A Farewell To Arms Crossword 2

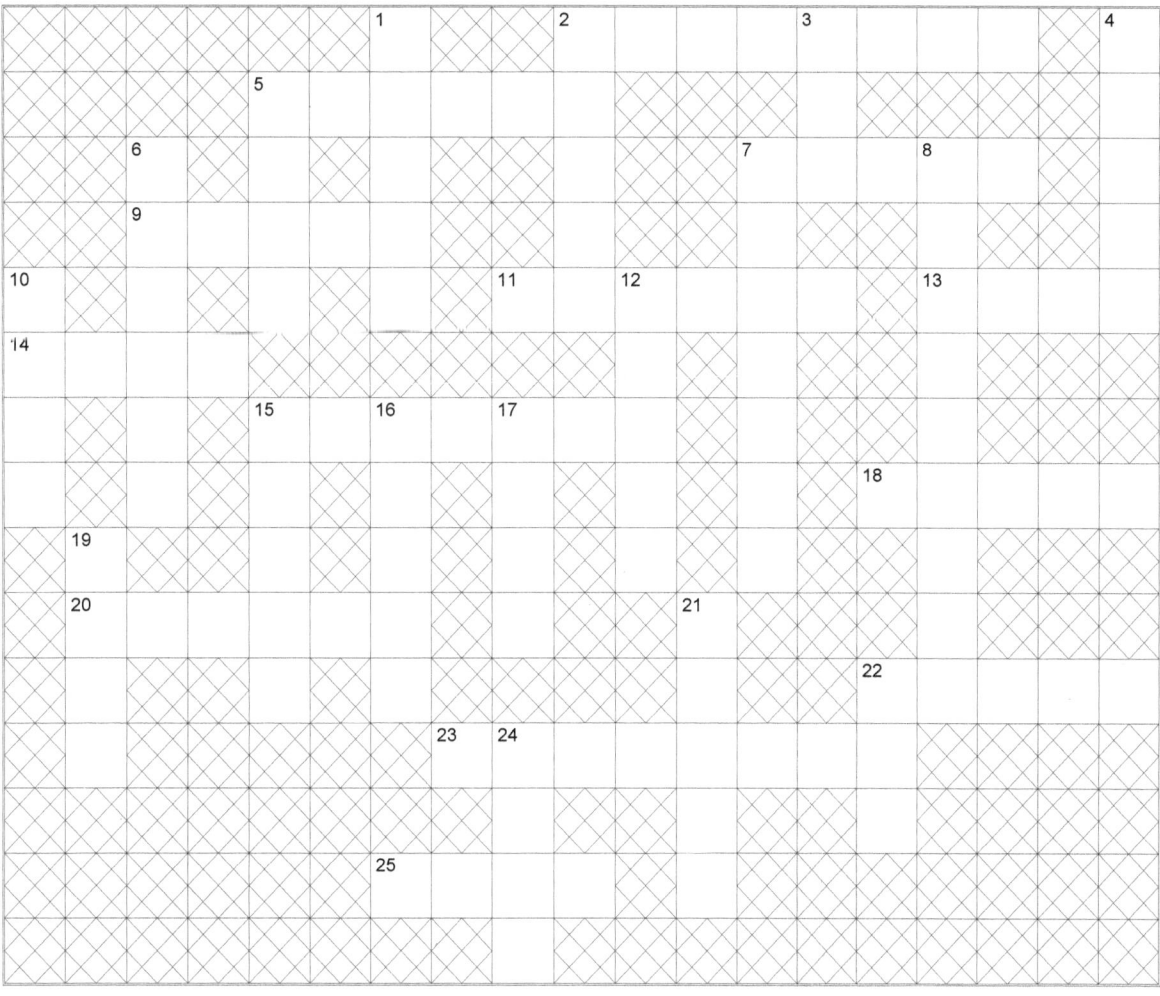

Across

2. A ___ To Arms
5. Frederick played billiards with him
7. A ___ person dies two thousand deaths but never mentions it
9. ___ was washed away in the river along with any obligation.
11. Catherine thinks he's boring
13. But ___ isn't hard to manage when you've nothing to lose.
14. Name of the mountain range
15. He was going to marry Catherine before Frederick met her.
18. Place where story takes place
20. They must be obeyed
22. ___ For Me; horse they bet on
23. Frederick's illness from drinking
25. Was shot by mistake by Italians

Down

1. Narrator: Frederick _____
2. In war, one side ____s the other
3. World ___ I
4. I am the ___. I am the ___ of reason.
5. Friend to Frederick and Catherine
6. Hospital supervisor; Van ____
7. Catherine's last name
8. A true Hemingway man; fixed Frederick's knee
10. Catherine is afraid of it
12. I'm not a bit afraid. It's just a dirty ___.
15. Place Frederick jumped into to escape
16. Catherine's profession
17. Feeling of Frederick towards Catherine
19. The barman gives Frederick & Catherine a ___ and food
21. Award
22. Where Frederick was wounded
24. A Farewell to ___

A Farewell To Arms Crossword 2 Answer Key

				1 H		2 F	A	R	3 E	W	E	L	L	4 S
			5 G	R	E	F	F	I			A			N
		6 C	A		N		G		7 B		8 V	E		A
		9 A	N	G	E	R		H	A		A			K
10 R		M	E		Y		11 E	12 T	T	O	R	E	13 L	I	F	E
14 A	L	P	S					R		K			E	
I		E		15 R	16 I	17 L	D	I		L		18 I	T	A	L	Y
N		N		I	U	O		C		E		T		
	19 B			V	R	V		K		Y		I		
	20 O	R	D	E	R	S		E		21 M		N		
	A			R		E				E		22 L	I	G	H	T
	T				23 J	24 A	U	N	D	I	C	E	
					R		A			G		
				25 A	Y	M	O		L			
					S							

Across
2. A ___ To Arms
5. Frederick played billiards with him
7. A ___ person dies two thousand deaths but never mentions it
9. ___ was washed away in the river along with any obligation.
11. Catherine thinks he's boring
13. But ___ isn't hard to manage when you've nothing to lose.
14. Name of the mountain range
15. He was going to marry Catherine before Frederick met her.
18. Place where story takes place
20. They must be obeyed
22. ___ For Me; horse they bet on
23. Frederick's illness from drinking
25. Was shot by mistake by Italians

Down
1. Narrator: Frederick _____
2. In war, one side ____s the other
3. World ___ I
4. I am the ___. I am the ___ of reason.
5. Friend to Frederick and Catherine
6. Hospital supervisor; Van ____
7. Catherine's last name
8. A true Hemingway man; fixed Frederick's knee
10. Catherine is afraid of it
12. I'm not a bit afraid. It's just a dirty ___.
15. Place Frederick jumped into to escape
16. Catherine's profession
17. Feeling of Frederick towards Catherine
19. The barman gives Frederick & Catherine a ___ and food
21. Award
22. Where Frederick was wounded
24. A Farewell to ___

A Farewell To Arms Crossword 3

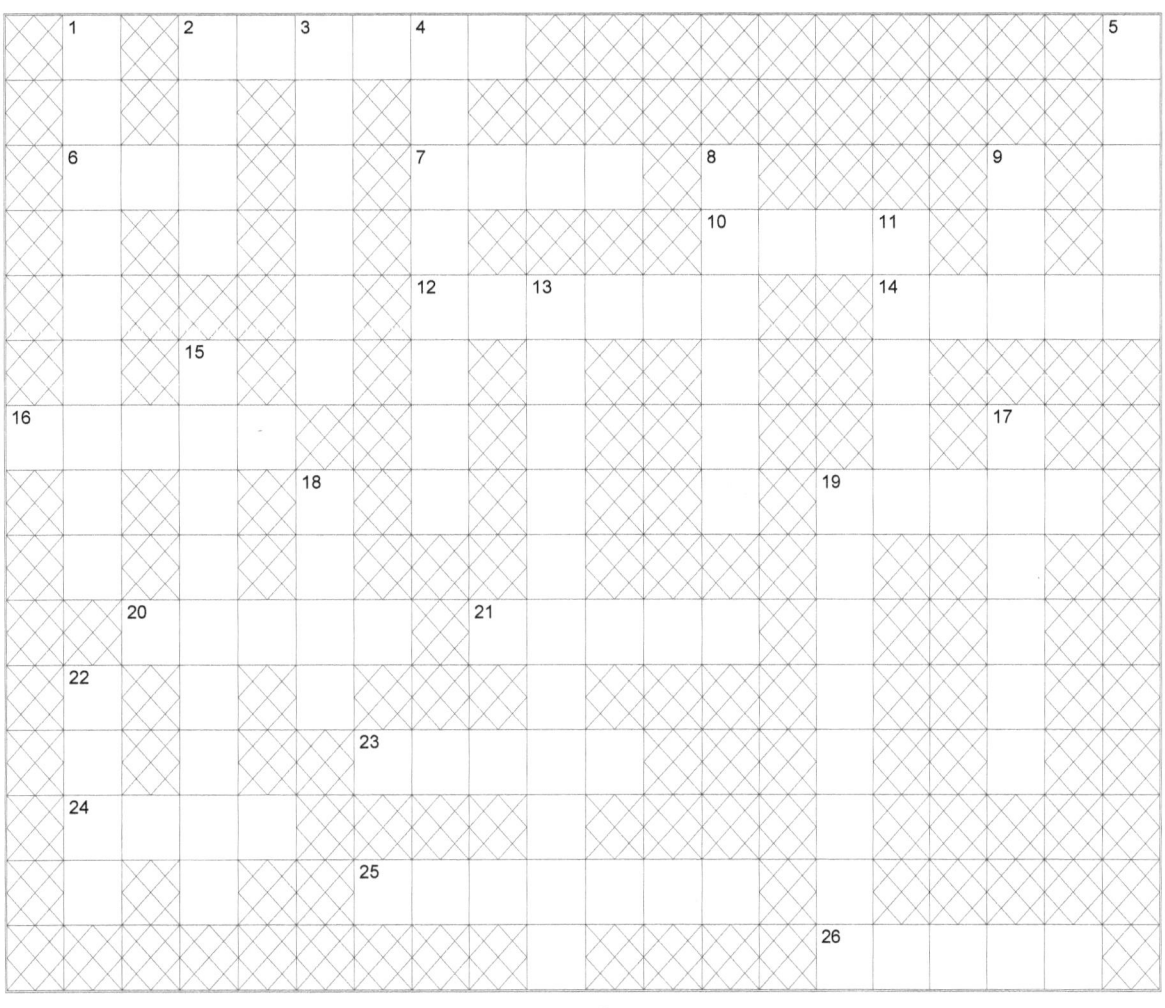

Across
2. Frederick played billiards with him
6. Where Frederick was wounded
7. Catherine is afraid of it
10. A Farewell to ___
12. Dear boy, that's not ___. That is cynicism.
14. Catherine's profession
16. Place Frederick jumped into to escape
19. Narrator: Frederick _____
20. ___ was washed away in the river along with any obligation.
21. I was going to forget the war. I had made a separate ___.
23. Place where story takes place
24. The barman gives Frederick & Catherine a ___ and food
25. Hurt but not killed
26. ___ For Me; horse they bet on

Down
1. A true Hemingway man; fixed Frederick's knee
2. Friend to Frederick and Catherine
3. Catherine thinks he's boring
4. A ___ To Arms
5. A ___ person dies two thousand deaths but never mentions it
8. Hospital supervisor; Van ____
9. World ___ I
11. I am the ___. I am the ___ of reason.
13. The neutral country
15. Author
17. They must be obeyed
18. It would help keep the baby small
19. Place where sick & wounded people are treated
22. It was born dead

A Farewell To Arms Crossword 3 Answer Key

	1 V	2 G	R	3 E	F	4 F	I						5 B
	A	A		T		A							R
	6 L	E	G		7 T	R	A	I	N	8 C		9 W	A
	E	E			O					10 A	R	M	S	A	V
	N			12 W	I	13 S	D	O	M		14 N	U	R	S	E
	T	15 H		E		W			P		A		
16 R	I	V	E	R		I			E		K	17 O	
	N	M		18 B	L	T			N	19 H	E	N	R	Y
	I	I		E		Z				O		D	
		20 A	N	G	E	R		21 P	E	A	C	E		E
	22 B	G		R				R		S		R
	A	W		23 I	T	A	L	Y		P		S
	24 B	O	A	T				A		I	
	Y	Y		25 W	O	U	N	D	E	D	
						D				26 L	I	G	H	T

Across
2. Frederick played billiards with him
6. Where Frederick was wounded
7. Catherine is afraid of it
10. A Farewell to ___
12. Dear boy, that's not ___. That is cynicism.
14. Catherine's profession
16. Place Frederick jumped into to escape
19. Narrator: Frederick _____
20. ___ was washed away in the river along with any obligation.
21. I was going to forget the war. I had made a separate ___.
23. Place where story takes place
24. The barman gives Frederick & Catherine a ___ and food
25. Hurt but not killed
26. ___ For Me; horse they bet on

Down
1. A true Hemingway man; fixed Frederick's knee
2. Friend to Frederick and Catherine
3. Catherine thinks he's boring
4. A ___ To Arms
5. A ___ person dies two thousand deaths but never mentions it
8. Hospital supervisor; Van ____
9. World ___ I
11. I am the ___. I am the ___ of reason.
13. The neutral country
15. Author
17. They must be obeyed
18. It would help keep the baby small
19. Place where sick & wounded people are treated
22. It was born dead

A Farewell To Arms Crossword 4

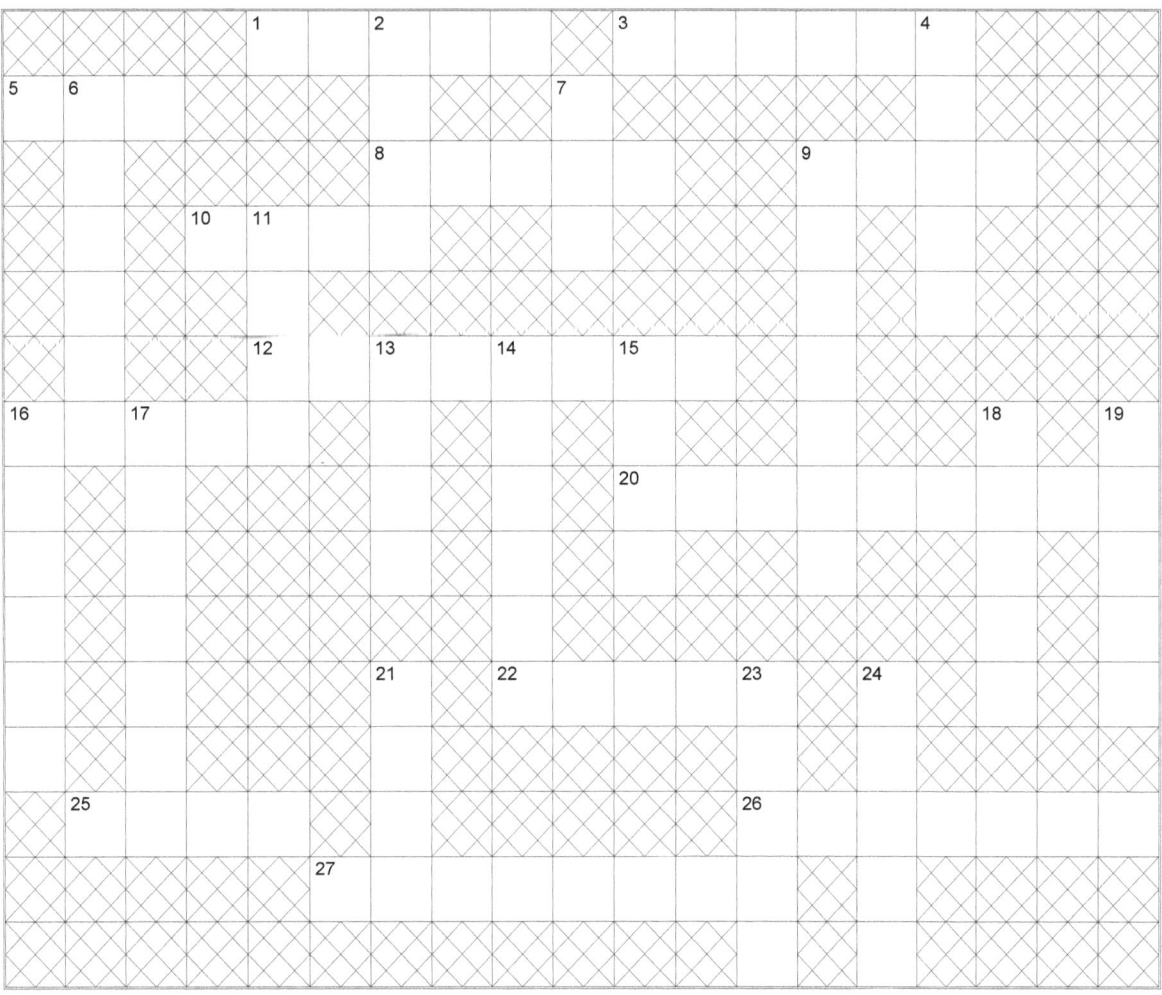

Across
1. A ___ person dies two thousand deaths but never mentions it
3. Frederick played billiards with him
5. Where Frederick was wounded
8. Award
9. The barman gives Frederick & Catherine a ___ and food
10. Name of the mountain range
12. A ___ To Arms
16. I was going to forget the war. I had made a separate ___.
20. A true Hemingway man; fixed Frederick's knee
22. Hospital where Catherine was transferred
25. Was shot by mistake by Italians
26. He was going to marry Catherine before Frederick met her.
27. Rinaldi said he and Frederick were alike underneath; like ___.

Down
2. A Farewell to ___
4. Place where story takes place
6. Catherine thinks he's boring
7. World ___ I
9. Catherine's last name
11. But ___ isn't hard to manage when you've nothing to lose.
13. Catherine is afraid of it
14. Dear boy, that's not ___. That is cynicism.
15. Feeling of Frederick towards Catherine
16. Rinaldi teases him, but Frederick shows some respect.
17. Catherine gave Frederick a St. ___ medal.
18. ___ For Me; horse they bet on
19. In war, one side ___s the other
21. It would help keep the baby small
23. Catherine's profession
24. Narrator: Frederick _____

43
Copyrighted

A Farewell To Arms Crossword 4 Answer Key

			¹B	²R	A	V	E		³G	R	E	F	F	⁴I		
⁵L	⁶E			R				⁷W						T		
	T			⁸M	E	D	A	L				⁹B	O	A	T	
	T		¹⁰A	¹¹L	P	S		R				A		L		
	O			I								R		Y		
	R			¹²F	¹³A	R	¹⁴E	W	¹⁵E	L	L		K			
¹⁶P	E	¹⁷A	C	E			I		O					¹⁸L	¹⁹F	
R		N					S		²⁰V	A	L	E	N	T	I	N I
I		T					D		E					G		G
E		H					O							H		H
S		O			²¹B	²²M	I	L	²³A	N		²⁴H		T		T
T		N			E				N			U		E		
	²⁵A	Y	M	O		E					²⁶R	I	N	A	L	D I
					²⁷B	R	O	T	H	E	R	S		R		
						E						E		Y		

Across
1. A ___ person dies two thousand deaths but never mentions it
3. Frederick played billiards with him
5. Where Frederick was wounded
8. Award
9. The barman gives Frederick & Catherine a ___ and food
10. Name of the mountain range
12. A ___ To Arms
16. I was going to forget the war. I had made a separate ___.
20. A true Hemingway man; fixed Frederick's knee
22. Hospital where Catherine was transferred
25. Was shot by mistake by Italians
26. He was going to marry Catherine before Frederick met her.
27. Rinaldi said he and Frederick were alike underneath; like ___.

Down
2. A Farewell to ___
4. Place where story takes place
6. Catherine thinks he's boring
7. World ___ I
9. Catherine's last name
11. But ___ isn't hard to manage when you've nothing to lose.
13. Catherine is afraid of it
14. Dear boy, that's not ___. That is cynicism.
15. Feeling of Frederick towards Catherine
16. Rinaldi teases him, but Frederick shows some respect.
17. Catherine gave Frederick a St. ___ medal.
18. ___ For Me; horse they bet on
19. In war, one side ____s the other
21. It would help keep the baby small
23. Catherine's profession
24. Narrator: Frederick _____

Farewell To Arms

BONELLO	ALPS	HEMINGWAY	CAMPEN	PEACE
BRAVE	GREFFI	SWITZERLAND	BEER	WISDOM
GAGE	WOUNDED	FREE SPACE	WAR	HOSPITAL
ANGER	PREGNANT	RAIN	LOVE	ARMS
RIVER	RINALDI	MEDAL	LIFE	BARMAN

Farewell To Arms

ITALY	NEWSPAPERS	ETTORE	MILAN	LEG
AYMO	ANTHONY	BOAT	AMBULANCE	TRICK
PRIEST	SNAKE	FREE SPACE	AMERICAN	HEMORRHAGES
HENRY	FAREWELL	FIGHT	NURSE	LIGHT
ORDERS	BROTHERS	VALENTINI	BABY	BARMAN

Farewell To Arms

MEDAL	LEG	RINALDI	ARMS	HOSPITAL
AMERICAN	BARMAN	HEMORRHAGES	ORDERS	BARKLEY
WOUNDED	WAR	FREE SPACE	PRIEST	AMBULANCE
PEACE	TRICK	NEWSPAPERS	RIVER	ANTHONY
BONELLO	GREFFI	LIFE	FAREWELL	LIGHT

Farewell To Arms

NURSE	SNAKE	VALENTINI	HENRY	BEER
BROTHERS	GAGE	WISDOM	AYMO	PREGNANT
ANGER	ITALY	FREE SPACE	ETTORE	BOAT
LOVE	HEMINGWAY	RAIN	MILAN	BRAVE
SWITZERLAND	ALPS	BABY	FIGHT	LIGHT

Farewell To Arms

FIGHT	AMBULANCE	HEMINGWAY	WOUNDED	BARMAN
LIFE	GAGE	GREFFI	AYMO	LIGHT
RIVER	WAR	FREE SPACE	RINALDI	LOVE
ARMS	ORDERS	ANTHONY	NURSE	TRICK
SWITZERLAND	ALPS	BROTHERS	RAIN	BRAVE

Farewell To Arms

PEACE	ITALY	LEG	HEMORRHAGES	VALENTINI
WISDOM	PRIEST	BOAT	SNAKE	NEWSPAPERS
BEER	CAMPEN	FREE SPACE	ANGER	ETTORE
MEDAL	JAUNDICE	BONELLO	BABY	HENRY
BARKLEY	MILAN	AMERICAN	HOSPITAL	BRAVE

Farewell To Arms

VALENTINI	ALPS	GAGE	BRAVE	BABY
JAUNDICE	NEWSPAPERS	MILAN	LEG	SWITZERLAND
ARMS	PREGNANT	FREE SPACE	BONELLO	AMBULANCE
AMERICAN	ITALY	AYMO	PRIEST	LOVE
FIGHT	ORDERS	MEDAL	GREFFI	ETTORE

Farewell To Arms

RINALDI	PEACE	BEER	HEMINGWAY	HEMORRHAGES
HENRY	FAREWELL	SNAKE	BOAT	WAR
CAMPEN	WOUNDED	FREE SPACE	WISDOM	HOSPITAL
BROTHERS	NURSE	ANGER	ANTHONY	LIFE
RIVER	RAIN	TRICK	LIGHT	ETTORE

Farewell To Arms

JAUNDICE	GAGE	ANTHONY	MEDAL	GREFFI
ALPS	MILAN	WAR	BABY	SWITZERLAND
NEWSPAPERS	PREGNANT	FREE SPACE	LOVE	RAIN
ITALY	WISDOM	BONELLO	ARMS	TRICK
HOSPITAL	BARKLEY	BOAT	ORDERS	AMBULANCE

Farewell To Arms

PRIEST	LIGHT	WOUNDED	FIGHT	HEMINGWAY
BARMAN	RINALDI	AYMO	ETTORE	LIFE
BEER	LEG	FREE SPACE	ANGER	AMERICAN
FAREWELL	NURSE	VALENTINI	BROTHERS	HEMORRHAGES
RIVER	HENRY	BRAVE	PEACE	AMBULANCE

Farewell To Arms

BARKLEY	ORDERS	RIVER	BEER	GREFFI
WISDOM	BROTHERS	AMBULANCE	PREGNANT	HEMINGWAY
ANGER	MILAN	FREE SPACE	ALPS	BABY
FIGHT	FAREWELL	SWITZERLAND	NURSE	HEMORRHAGES
GAGE	ITALY	CAMPEN	ARMS	WOUNDED

Farewell To Arms

HOSPITAL	WAR	BRAVE	MEDAL	LEG
PRIEST	TRICK	LIFE	PEACE	BONELLO
LOVE	BOAT	FREE SPACE	JAUNDICE	RINALDI
HENRY	BARMAN	ETTORE	NEWSPAPERS	SNAKE
VALENTINI	AMERICAN	LIGHT	RAIN	WOUNDED

Farewell To Arms

HEMORRHAGES	AMBULANCE	TRICK	SWITZERLAND	FIGHT
WISDOM	RIVER	BABY	LOVE	AYMO
ETTORE	NEWSPAPERS	FREE SPACE	BROTHERS	RAIN
CAMPEN	NURSE	BARMAN	GAGE	ITALY
AMERICAN	GREFFI	ALPS	LEG	MEDAL

Farewell To Arms

BOAT	BRAVE	ANGER	ORDERS	JAUNDICE
VALENTINI	BONELLO	SNAKE	ARMS	RINALDI
FAREWELL	HEMINGWAY	FREE SPACE	WOUNDED	PRIEST
BARKLEY	MILAN	WAR	HENRY	HOSPITAL
BEER	LIFE	PEACE	ANTHONY	MEDAL

Farewell To Arms

ANGER	ARMS	BARKLEY	NEWSPAPERS	HOSPITAL
ITALY	JAUNDICE	LIGHT	RINALDI	SWITZERLAND
AMERICAN	AYMO	FREE SPACE	FAREWELL	MEDAL
LOVE	ETTORE	HEMORRHAGES	LIFE	TRICK
FIGHT	ORDERS	BOAT	WOUNDED	BEER

Farewell To Arms

WISDOM	BROTHERS	GAGE	CAMPEN	VALENTINI
PEACE	NURSE	LEG	RIVER	RAIN
ALPS	BARMAN	FREE SPACE	PREGNANT	BRAVE
GREFFI	WAR	HEMINGWAY	PRIEST	SNAKE
BONELLO	ANTHONY	HENRY	BABY	BEER

Farewell To Arms

ITALY	LEG	RAIN	HEMORRHAGES	MILAN
PRIEST	GAGE	AYMO	FIGHT	SWITZERLAND
BROTHERS	BARMAN	FREE SPACE	LOVE	ETTORE
HOSPITAL	ANTHONY	HENRY	NEWSPAPERS	AMERICAN
BONELLO	GREFFI	SNAKE	AMBULANCE	BEER

Farewell To Arms

WISDOM	FAREWELL	RINALDI	JAUNDICE	ALPS
LIGHT	RIVER	MEDAL	LIFE	ANGER
HEMINGWAY	WOUNDED	FREE SPACE	BRAVE	ORDERS
WAR	BABY	TRICK	NURSE	CAMPEN
ARMS	PREGNANT	VALENTINI	BOAT	BEER

Farewell To Arms

FAREWELL	BROTHERS	ETTORE	MEDAL	ALPS
ORDERS	RAIN	GAGE	CAMPEN	AMERICAN
BARMAN	BRAVE	FREE SPACE	RIVER	LOVE
RINALDI	ANGER	WOUNDED	SWITZERLAND	VALENTINI
PREGNANT	AYMO	HEMORRHAGES	HOSPITAL	GREFFI

Farewell To Arms

BARKLEY	SNAKE	BOAT	ANTHONY	FIGHT
LIGHT	HEMINGWAY	WAR	MILAN	ARMS
BEER	NEWSPAPERS	FREE SPACE	NURSE	BONELLO
PRIEST	JAUNDICE	BABY	LIFE	TRICK
HENRY	PEACE	ITALY	LEG	GREFFI

Farewell To Arms

WAR	BARMAN	PRIEST	BEER	HENRY
NEWSPAPERS	BRAVE	FAREWELL	HOSPITAL	PREGNANT
CAMPEN	BROTHERS	FREE SPACE	FIGHT	JAUNDICE
LOVE	AMBULANCE	HEMORRHAGES	BABY	ALPS
MEDAL	VALENTINI	BARKLEY	GAGE	LIFE

Farewell To Arms

WOUNDED	HEMINGWAY	WISDOM	SNAKE	AMERICAN
SWITZERLAND	AYMO	ANGER	ETTORE	RIVER
LIGHT	ANTHONY	FREE SPACE	BONELLO	MILAN
RAIN	RINALDI	ORDERS	PEACE	TRICK
LEG	ARMS	ITALY	GREFFI	LIFE

Farewell To Arms

PRIEST	ANGER	ANTHONY	TRICK	GREFFI
HEMORRHAGES	FAREWELL	ITALY	BOAT	LOVE
HEMINGWAY	VALENTINI	FREE SPACE	BABY	BRAVE
MEDAL	ORDERS	LEG	AYMO	FIGHT
JAUNDICE	LIGHT	ALPS	NURSE	LIFE

Farewell To Arms

MILAN	NEWSPAPERS	WOUNDED	BROTHERS	BARMAN
BONELLO	WISDOM	CAMPEN	PEACE	BARKLEY
SNAKE	WAR	FREE SPACE	AMERICAN	RAIN
SWITZERLAND	PREGNANT	HENRY	ETTORE	RINALDI
GAGE	ARMS	BEER	RIVER	LIFE

Farewell To Arms

LIGHT	LEG	PEACE	FAREWELL	BEER
GREFFI	HEMORRHAGES	ANTHONY	SWITZERLAND	CAMPEN
SNAKE	PRIEST	FREE SPACE	AMBULANCE	BARMAN
GAGE	BRAVE	HEMINGWAY	HENRY	WAR
BROTHERS	JAUNDICE	NEWSPAPERS	ITALY	ALPS

Farewell To Arms

BONELLO	MILAN	AMERICAN	WISDOM	BARKLEY
FIGHT	AYMO	ANGER	WOUNDED	ARMS
VALENTINI	BABY	FREE SPACE	LIFE	PREGNANT
ETTORE	MEDAL	BOAT	HOSPITAL	TRICK
RAIN	LOVE	NURSE	ORDERS	ALPS

Farewell To Arms

HEMINGWAY	LOVE	ANGER	HENRY	BROTHERS
RIVER	JAUNDICE	BARMAN	VALENTINI	PRIEST
ARMS	FAREWELL	FREE SPACE	ANTHONY	PREGNANT
GAGE	ORDERS	NURSE	AMBULANCE	ETTORE
FIGHT	AYMO	BONELLO	LIGHT	BEER

Farewell To Arms

WISDOM	NEWSPAPERS	GREFFI	SWITZERLAND	AMERICAN
RINALDI	LEG	MEDAL	TRICK	BABY
HEMORRHAGES	HOSPITAL	FREE SPACE	WOUNDED	SNAKE
LIFE	MILAN	WAR	CAMPEN	BRAVE
ALPS	BOAT	RAIN	ITALY	BEER

Farewell To Arms

BOAT	WOUNDED	BONELLO	LIFE	GREFFI
ETTORE	TRICK	VALENTINI	LEG	BRAVE
ORDERS	ALPS	FREE SPACE	PRIEST	BARMAN
HOSPITAL	SNAKE	ANTHONY	BARKLEY	PEACE
HEMINGWAY	JAUNDICE	LIGHT	MILAN	WISDOM

Farewell To Arms

BROTHERS	NEWSPAPERS	HENRY	BABY	ANGER
HEMORRHAGES	FIGHT	ITALY	NURSE	PREGNANT
CAMPEN	AYMO	FREE SPACE	SWITZERLAND	LOVE
FAREWELL	AMBULANCE	BEER	RAIN	MEDAL
ARMS	RIVER	GAGE	AMERICAN	WISDOM

Farewell To Arms

PEACE	LEG	BOAT	HEMINGWAY	BROTHERS
HENRY	JAUNDICE	LOVE	FIGHT	ETTORE
MEDAL	LIFE	FREE SPACE	SWITZERLAND	ARMS
BEER	NEWSPAPERS	SNAKE	FAREWELL	ANTHONY
BONELLO	ANGER	VALENTINI	AMERICAN	PRIEST

Farewell To Arms

HOSPITAL	BABY	WAR	GAGE	RINALDI
BARKLEY	RIVER	HEMORRHAGES	BRAVE	AMBULANCE
BARMAN	MILAN	FREE SPACE	PREGNANT	ALPS
NURSE	AYMO	CAMPEN	WISDOM	GREFFI
LIGHT	WOUNDED	TRICK	ITALY	PRIEST

A Farewell To Arms Vocabulary Word List

No.	Word	Clue/Definition
1.	AGITATORS	Protesters; troublemakers
2.	ANARCHIST	One who thinks government should be abandoned
3.	ARTICULATION	Connection; fitting together
4.	ARTILLERY	Large guns and cannons
5.	ATHEISTS	People who do not believe in God
6.	BATTERY	Unit of guns or other weapons
7.	BELLOWS	Shouts in a loud, deep voice
8.	BILE	Fluid produced in the liver
9.	BRITTLENESS	Being weak and likely to break or crack
10.	CAMIONS	Buses or trucks
11.	CHALET	Traditional Swiss wooden cottage
12.	CHOLERA	A disease of the intestines caused by bacteria
13.	CITATION	Official document of praise
14.	COAGULATES	Thickens; clots; sticks together
15.	COMMENCED	Started
16.	CONCEITED	Having a very high opinion of oneself
17.	CONSCIENTIOUSLY	Carefully; with thought; dutifully
18.	CONTEMPTUOUSLY	In a disapproving way
19.	CORDIAL	Pleasant; friendly
20.	CYNICISM	Negative sarcasm or mockery
21.	DECORATED	Given a medal or other honor
22.	DEVOUT	Very religious
23.	DISMAL	Gloomy; depressing
24.	DOMINEERING	Bossy or controlling
25.	DORMER	Window built at right angles to the roof
26.	DRESSING	Bandages & things pertaining to treating wounds
27.	ELATED	Happy and excited
28.	EMERY	Sandpaper
29.	EVACUATES	Leaves a dangerous place
30.	EXALTED	Praiseworthy
31.	EXHILARATION	Happiness and excitement
32.	FALLACY	Belief that is actually incorrect
33.	FORMALITIES	Official procedures that must be followed
34.	FRAGMENTS	Small pieces of something shattered
35.	FRONT	The leading position in a war
36.	GROGGY	Weak or dizzy; not fully alert
37.	GUSTS	Sudden, violent bursts of wind
38.	GYPS	Cheats out of money
39.	HEMORRHAGE	Bleeding; a loss of blood
40.	HOSTILE	Unfriendly; showing hatred toward another
41.	IMPARTIALLY	Fairly
42.	INFANTRY	Soldiers who fight on foot
43.	INTERN	Put in prison
44.	INVIGORATING	Filling with energy
45.	LEGITIMATE	Legal; lawful
46.	MATRONLY	Like a mature woman with sensible qualities
47.	NUISANCE	Annoyance; irritation
48.	OBSCENE	Morally offensive
49.	OBSTACLES	Things that get in the way or stop progress
50.	OFFENSIVE	An attack or assault

A Farewell To Arms Vocabulary Word List Cont.

No.	Word	Clue/Definition
51.	PORTER	One who is hired to carry baggage
52.	PROJECTILE	Bullet; shell
53.	PROTRACTED	Lasting for a long time
54.	PRY	Force apart or open with a lever
55.	PUNCTURE	Reduce someone's confidence
56.	REFRAINED	Held back; kept from doing
57.	REGIMENT	A grouping of military troops
58.	REMORSE	Strong feeling of guilt or sorrow
59.	RIDGE	Long, narrow hilltop
60.	RUCKSACK	Backpack
61.	RUPTURE	A tear in tissue in the body; a hernia
62.	SCARCE	In short or limited supply
63.	SCRUTINIZING	Examining carefully
64.	SECTOR	Zone; division
65.	SENTIMENT	Thoughts based on feelings
66.	SHEDS	Causes water to flow or drop off
67.	SOCIALISTS	People who believe in control by the people
68.	SOLEMN	Serious; humorless
69.	SQUABBLED	Argued
70.	STRAINED	Full of tension; nervous
71.	TAUT	Tense; tight
72.	TORRENT	Fast, powerful flood of water
73.	TOURNIQUET	Tight band used to stop bleeding
74.	TRAJECTORY	Route; path
75.	TRUSS	Medical device used to support a hernia
76.	UNCHAPERONED	Not accompanied by a supervisor
77.	UNGAINLY	Clumsy; not graceful
78.	VAGUE	Not clear in meaning

A Farewell To Arms Vocabulary Fill In The Blanks 1

1. Bleeding; a loss of blood
2. Happy and excited
3. Causes water to flow or drop off
4. Connection; fitting together
5. People who do not believe in God
6. Small pieces of something shattered
7. Sudden, violent bursts of wind
8. Backpack
9. Put in prison
10. Thoughts based on feelings
11. Legal; lawful
12. Buses or trucks
13. Argued
14. Weak or dizzy; not fully alert
15. Thickens; clots; sticks together
16. Like a mature woman with sensible qualities
17. Official procedures that must be followed
18. The leading position in a war
19. Fairly
20. Filling with energy

A Farewell To Arms Vocabulary Fill In The Blanks 1 Answer Key

HEMORRHAGE	1. Bleeding; a loss of blood
ELATED	2. Happy and excited
SHEDS	3. Causes water to flow or drop off
ARTICULATION	4. Connection; fitting together
ATHEISTS	5. People who do not believe in God
FRAGMENTS	6. Small pieces of something shattered
GUSTS	7. Sudden, violent bursts of wind
RUCKSACK	8. Backpack
INTERN	9. Put in prison
SENTIMENT	10. Thoughts based on feelings
LEGITIMATE	11. Legal; lawful
CAMIONS	12. Buses or trucks
SQUABBLED	13. Argued
GROGGY	14. Weak or dizzy; not fully alert
COAGULATES	15. Thickens; clots; sticks together
MATRONLY	16. Like a mature woman with sensible qualities
FORMALITIES	17. Official procedures that must be followed
FRONT	18. The leading position in a war
IMPARTIALLY	19. Fairly
INVIGORATING	20. Filling with energy

A Farewell To Arms Vocabulary Fill In The Blanks 2

_____ 1. Put in prison

_____ 2. An attack or assault

_____ 3. Examining carefully

_____ 4. Reduce someone's confidence

_____ 5. Happy and excited

_____ 6. Bleeding; a loss of blood

_____ 7. Fluid produced in the liver

_____ 8. Thoughts based on feelings

_____ 9. Force apart or open with a lever

_____ 10. Full of tension; nervous

_____ 11. Official document of praise

_____ 12. Filling with energy

_____ 13. Protesters; troublemakers

_____ 14. In a disapproving way

_____ 15. Official procedures that must be followed

_____ 16. Zone; division

_____ 17. Tense; tight

_____ 18. Not clear in meaning

_____ 19. One who is hired to carry baggage

_____ 20. Morally offensive

A Farewell To Arms Vocabulary Fill In The Blanks 2 Answer Key

INTERN	1. Put in prison
OFFENSIVE	2. An attack or assault
SCRUTINIZING	3. Examining carefully
PUNCTURE	4. Reduce someone's confidence
ELATED	5. Happy and excited
HEMORRHAGE	6. Bleeding; a loss of blood
BILE	7. Fluid produced in the liver
SENTIMENT	8. Thoughts based on feelings
PRY	9. Force apart or open with a lever
STRAINED	10. Full of tension; nervous
CITATION	11. Official document of praise
INVIGORATING	12. Filling with energy
AGITATORS	13. Protesters; troublemakers
CONTEMPTUOUSLY	14. In a disapproving way
FORMALITIES	15. Official procedures that must be followed
SECTOR	16. Zone; division
TAUT	17. Tense; tight
VAGUE	18. Not clear in meaning
PORTER	19. One who is hired to carry baggage
OBSCENE	20. Morally offensive

A Farewell To Arms Vocabulary Fill In The Blanks 3

_____ 1. Route; path

_____ 2. Not accompanied by a supervisor

_____ 3. Long, narrow hilltop

_____ 4. Annoyance; irritation

_____ 5. Thoughts based on feelings

_____ 6. Medical device used to support a hernia

_____ 7. One who thinks government should be abandoned

_____ 8. In a disapproving way

_____ 9. Force apart or open with a lever

_____ 10. Fast, powerful flood of water

_____ 11. Bleeding; a loss of blood

_____ 12. In short or limited supply

_____ 13. Tense; tight

_____ 14. Tight band used to stop bleeding

_____ 15. Given a medal or other honor

_____ 16. Started

_____ 17. Held back; kept from doing

_____ 18. Gloomy; depressing

_____ 19. Fairly

_____ 20. Serious; humorless

A Farewell To Arms Vocabulary Fill In The Blanks 3 Answer Key

TRAJECTORY	1. Route; path
UNCHAPERONED	2. Not accompanied by a supervisor
RIDGE	3. Long, narrow hilltop
NUISANCE	4. Annoyance; irritation
SENTIMENT	5. Thoughts based on feelings
TRUSS	6. Medical device used to support a hernia
ANARCHIST	7. One who thinks government should be abandoned
CONTEMPTUOUSLY	8. In a disapproving way
PRY	9. Force apart or open with a lever
TORRENT	10. Fast, powerful flood of water
HEMORRHAGE	11. Bleeding; a loss of blood
SCARCE	12. In short or limited supply
TAUT	13. Tense; tight
TOURNIQUET	14. Tight band used to stop bleeding
DECORATED	15. Given a medal or other honor
COMMENCED	16. Started
REFRAINED	17. Held back; kept from doing
DISMAL	18. Gloomy; depressing
IMPARTIALLY	19. Fairly
SOLEMN	20. Serious; humorless

A Farewell To Arms Vocabulary Fill In The Blanks 4

_____ 1. Morally offensive

_____ 2. Tight band used to stop bleeding

_____ 3. Cheats out of money

_____ 4. Strong feeling of guilt or sorrow

_____ 5. Carefully; with thought; dutifully

_____ 6. Long, narrow hilltop

_____ 7. Legal; lawful

_____ 8. In short or limited supply

_____ 9. People who do not believe in God

_____ 10. Not accompanied by a supervisor

_____ 11. Sudden, violent bursts of wind

_____ 12. In a disapproving way

_____ 13. Argued

_____ 14. Bossy or controlling

_____ 15. Protesters; troublemakers

_____ 16. Official document of praise

_____ 17. Examining carefully

_____ 18. Small pieces of something shattered

_____ 19. Not clear in meaning

_____ 20. Thoughts based on feelings

A Farewell To Arms Vocabulary Fill In The Blanks 4 Answer Key

OBSCENE	1. Morally offensive
TOURNIQUET	2. Tight band used to stop bleeding
GYPS	3. Cheats out of money
REMORSE	4. Strong feeling of guilt or sorrow
CONSCIENTIOUSLY	5. Carefully; with thought; dutifully
RIDGE	6. Long, narrow hilltop
LEGITIMATE	7. Legal; lawful
SCARCE	8. In short or limited supply
ATHEISTS	9. People who do not believe in God
UNCHAPERONED	10. Not accompanied by a supervisor
GUSTS	11. Sudden, violent bursts of wind
CONTEMPTUOUSLY	12. In a disapproving way
SQUABBLED	13. Argued
DOMINEERING	14. Bossy or controlling
AGITATORS	15. Protesters; troublemakers
CITATION	16. Official document of praise
SCRUTINIZING	17. Examining carefully
FRAGMENTS	18. Small pieces of something shattered
VAGUE	19. Not clear in meaning
SENTIMENT	20. Thoughts based on feelings

A Farewell To Arms Vocabulary Matching 1

___ 1. SHEDS				A. Filling with energy
___ 2. RUPTURE			B. Serious; humorless
___ 3. REFRAINED			C. Medical device used to support a hernia
___ 4. DOMINEERING		D. Examining carefully
___ 5. HOSTILE			E. A grouping of military troops
___ 6. EXHILARATION		F. Lasting for a long time
___ 7. REGIMENT			G. Thickens; clots; sticks together
___ 8. COAGULATES		H. Causes water to flow or drop off
___ 9. IMPARTIALLY		I. Having a very high opinion of oneself
___ 10. ARTICULATION		J. Held back; kept from doing
___ 11. VAGUE			K. Connection; fitting together
___ 12. ELATED			L. Bossy or controlling
___ 13. SCRUTINIZING		M. Force apart or open with a lever
___ 14. PRY				N. Happy and excited
___ 15. PORTER			O. Happiness and excitement
___ 16. INVIGORATING		P. Fairly
___ 17. SOLEMN			Q. Small pieces of something shattered
___ 18. EXALTED			R. Unfriendly; showing hatred toward another
___ 19. FRAGMENTS		S. Not clear in meaning
___ 20. DEVOUT			T. Very religious
___ 21. AGITATORS		U. One who is hired to carry baggage
___ 22. TAUT			V. A tear in tissue in the body; a hernia
___ 23. CONCEITED		W. Tense; tight
___ 24. PROTRACTED		X. Protesters; troublemakers
___ 25. TRUSS			Y. Praiseworthy

A Farewell To Arms Vocabulary Matching 1 Answer Key

H - 1.	SHEDS	A. Filling with energy
V - 2.	RUPTURE	B. Serious; humorless
J - 3.	REFRAINED	C. Medical device used to support a hernia
L - 4.	DOMINEERING	D. Examining carefully
R - 5.	HOSTILE	E. A grouping of military troops
O - 6.	EXHILARATION	F. Lasting for a long time
E - 7.	REGIMENT	G. Thickens; clots; sticks together
G - 8.	COAGULATES	H. Causes water to flow or drop off
P - 9.	IMPARTIALLY	I. Having a very high opinion of oneself
K - 10.	ARTICULATION	J. Held back; kept from doing
S - 11.	VAGUE	K. Connection; fitting together
N - 12.	ELATED	L. Bossy or controlling
D - 13.	SCRUTINIZING	M. Force apart or open with a lever
M - 14.	PRY	N. Happy and excited
U - 15.	PORTER	O. Happiness and excitement
A - 16.	INVIGORATING	P. Fairly
B - 17.	SOLEMN	Q. Small pieces of something shattered
Y - 18.	EXALTED	R. Unfriendly; showing hatred toward another
Q - 19.	FRAGMENTS	S. Not clear in meaning
T - 20.	DEVOUT	T. Very religious
X - 21.	AGITATORS	U. One who is hired to carry baggage
W - 22.	TAUT	V. A tear in tissue in the body; a hernia
I - 23.	CONCEITED	W. Tense; tight
F - 24.	PROTRACTED	X. Protesters; troublemakers
C - 25.	TRUSS	Y. Praiseworthy

A Farewell To Arms Vocabulary Matching 2

___ 1. GROGGY   A. Causes water to flow or drop off
___ 2. CYNICISM   B. Weak or dizzy; not fully alert
___ 3. SOCIALISTS   C. Thickens; clots; sticks together
___ 4. HEMORRHAGE   D. Sudden, violent bursts of wind
___ 5. OFFENSIVE   E. In short or limited supply
___ 6. DECORATED   F. Very religious
___ 7. GUSTS   G. People who believe in control by the people
___ 8. CITATION   H. Long, narrow hilltop
___ 9. PRY   I. Having a very high opinion of oneself
___ 10. INVIGORATING   J. Connection; fitting together
___ 11. EXHILARATION   K. Given a medal or other honor
___ 12. DOMINEERING   L. Official document of praise
___ 13. VAGUE   M. Tense; tight
___ 14. DORMER   N. Not clear in meaning
___ 15. SHEDS   O. Medical device used to support a hernia
___ 16. COAGULATES   P. Unit of guns or other weapons
___ 17. DEVOUT   Q. Happiness and excitement
___ 18. TRUSS   R. Force apart or open with a lever
___ 19. PROJECTILE   S. Bleeding; a loss of blood
___ 20. ARTICULATION   T. Bullet; shell
___ 21. CONCEITED   U. Negative sarcasm or mockery
___ 22. TAUT   V. Window built at right angles to the roof
___ 23. SCARCE   W. An attack or assault
___ 24. RIDGE   X. Filling with energy
___ 25. BATTERY   Y. Bossy or controlling

A Farewell To Arms Vocabulary Matching 2 Answer Key

B - 1. GROGGY	A.	Causes water to flow or drop off
U - 2. CYNICISM	B.	Weak or dizzy; not fully alert
G - 3. SOCIALISTS	C.	Thickens; clots; sticks together
S - 4. HEMORRHAGE	D.	Sudden, violent bursts of wind
W - 5. OFFENSIVE	E.	In short or limited supply
K - 6. DECORATED	F.	Very religious
D - 7. GUSTS	G.	People who believe in control by the people
L - 8. CITATION	H.	Long, narrow hilltop
R - 9. PRY	I.	Having a very high opinion of oneself
X - 10. INVIGORATING	J.	Connection; fitting together
Q - 11. EXHILARATION	K.	Given a medal or other honor
Y - 12. DOMINEERING	L.	Official document of praise
N - 13. VAGUE	M.	Tense; tight
V - 14. DORMER	N.	Not clear in meaning
A - 15. SHEDS	O.	Medical device used to support a hernia
C - 16. COAGULATES	P.	Unit of guns or other weapons
F - 17. DEVOUT	Q.	Happiness and excitement
O - 18. TRUSS	R.	Force apart or open with a lever
T - 19. PROJECTILE	S.	Bleeding; a loss of blood
J - 20. ARTICULATION	T.	Bullet; shell
I - 21. CONCEITED	U.	Negative sarcasm or mockery
M - 22. TAUT	V.	Window built at right angles to the roof
E - 23. SCARCE	W.	An attack or assault
H - 24. RIDGE	X.	Filling with energy
P - 25. BATTERY	Y.	Bossy or controlling

A Farewell To Arms Vocabulary Matching 3

___ 1. RIDGE   A. Fast, powerful flood of water
___ 2. EXHILARATION   B. Not clear in meaning
___ 3. OBSCENE   C. Strong feeling of guilt or sorrow
___ 4. CHOLERA   D. The leading position in a war
___ 5. DEVOUT   E. Argued
___ 6. SCRUTINIZING   F. Long, narrow hilltop
___ 7. CONCEITED   G. Having a very high opinion of oneself
___ 8. ARTICULATION   H. Fairly
___ 9. TORRENT   I. Very religious
___10. IMPARTIALLY   J. Zone; division
___11. SQUABBLED   K. A disease of the intestines caused by bacteria
___12. INVIGORATING   L. Praiseworthy
___13. SECTOR   M. Examining carefully
___14. REMORSE   N. Started
___15. OBSTACLES   O. Connection; fitting together
___16. VAGUE   P. Filling with energy
___17. DISMAL   Q. Gloomy; depressing
___18. SOCIALISTS   R. Pleasant; friendly
___19. PROTRACTED   S. Happy and excited
___20. COMMENCED   T. Morally offensive
___21. CHALET   U. Lasting for a long time
___22. FRONT   V. People who believe in control by the people
___23. CORDIAL   W. Traditional Swiss wooden cottage
___24. ELATED   X. Happiness and excitement
___25. EXALTED   Y. Things that get in the way or stop progress

A Farewell To Arms Vocabulary Matching 3 Answer Key

F - 1.	RIDGE	A. Fast, powerful flood of water
X - 2.	EXHILARATION	B. Not clear in meaning
T - 3.	OBSCENE	C. Strong feeling of guilt or sorrow
K - 4.	CHOLERA	D. The leading position in a war
I - 5.	DEVOUT	E. Argued
M - 6.	SCRUTINIZING	F. Long, narrow hilltop
G - 7.	CONCEITED	G. Having a very high opinion of oneself
O - 8.	ARTICULATION	H. Fairly
A - 9.	TORRENT	I. Very religious
H - 10.	IMPARTIALLY	J. Zone; division
E - 11.	SQUABBLED	K. A disease of the intestines caused by bacteria
P - 12.	INVIGORATING	L. Praiseworthy
J - 13.	SECTOR	M. Examining carefully
C - 14.	REMORSE	N. Started
Y - 15.	OBSTACLES	O. Connection; fitting together
B - 16.	VAGUE	P. Filling with energy
Q - 17.	DISMAL	Q. Gloomy; depressing
V - 18.	SOCIALISTS	R. Pleasant; friendly
U - 19.	PROTRACTED	S. Happy and excited
N - 20.	COMMENCED	T. Morally offensive
W - 21.	CHALET	U. Lasting for a long time
D - 22.	FRONT	V. People who believe in control by the people
R - 23.	CORDIAL	W. Traditional Swiss wooden cottage
S - 24.	ELATED	X. Happiness and excitement
L - 25.	EXALTED	Y. Things that get in the way or stop progress

A Farewell To Arms Vocabulary Matching 4

___ 1. TAUT   A. Reduce someone's confidence
___ 2. EXHILARATION   B. Carefully; with thought; dutifully
___ 3. CONSCIENTIOUSLY C. Shouts in a loud, deep voice
___ 4. SQUABBLED   D. Put in prison
___ 5. RUCKSACK   E. Serious; humorless
___ 6. TRUSS   F. Sandpaper
___ 7. PROJECTILE   G. Bullet; shell
___ 8. HEMORRHAGE   H. Annoyance; irritation
___ 9. CHALET   I. Official procedures that must be followed
___10. BELLOWS   J. Argued
___11. SOLEMN   K. Gloomy; depressing
___12. NUISANCE   L. Praiseworthy
___13. CYNICISM   M. Negative sarcasm or mockery
___14. PUNCTURE   N. The leading position in a war
___15. ARTILLERY   O. Tense; tight
___16. INTERN   P. Medical device used to support a hernia
___17. BRITTLENESS   Q. Bleeding; a loss of blood
___18. FRONT   R. Large guns and cannons
___19. OBSCENE   S. Traditional Swiss wooden cottage
___20. DISMAL   T. Happiness and excitement
___21. FORMALITIES   U. Examining carefully
___22. SCRUTINIZING   V. Thickens; clots; sticks together
___23. COAGULATES   W. Morally offensive
___24. EXALTED   X. Being weak and likely to break or crack
___25. EMERY   Y. Backpack

A Farewell To Arms Vocabulary Matching 4 Answer Key

O - 1. TAUT A. Reduce someone's confidence
T - 2. EXHILARATION B. Carefully; with thought; dutifully
B - 3. CONSCIENTIOUSLY C. Shouts in a loud, deep voice
J - 4. SQUABBLED D. Put in prison
Y - 5. RUCKSACK E. Serious; humorless
P - 6. TRUSS F. Sandpaper
G - 7. PROJECTILE G. Bullet; shell
Q - 8. HEMORRHAGE H. Annoyance; irritation
S - 9. CHALET I. Official procedures that must be followed
C - 10. BELLOWS J. Argued
E - 11. SOLEMN K. Gloomy; depressing
H - 12. NUISANCE L. Praiseworthy
M - 13. CYNICISM M. Negative sarcasm or mockery
A - 14. PUNCTURE N. The leading position in a war
R - 15. ARTILLERY O. Tense; tight
D - 16. INTERN P. Medical device used to support a hernia
X - 17. BRITTLENESS Q. Bleeding; a loss of blood
N - 18. FRONT R. Large guns and cannons
W - 19. OBSCENE S. Traditional Swiss wooden cottage
K - 20. DISMAL T. Happiness and excitement
I - 21. FORMALITIES U. Examining carefully
U - 22. SCRUTINIZING V. Thickens; clots; sticks together
V - 23. COAGULATES W. Morally offensive
L - 24. EXALTED X. Being weak and likely to break or crack
F - 25. EMERY Y. Backpack

A Farewell To Arms Vocabulary Magic Squares 1

A. DEVOUT
B. PUNCTURE
C. SCRUTINIZING
D. REMORSE
E. CAMIONS
F. VAGUE
G. INTERN
H. PROJECTILE
I. TOURNIQUET
J. CONCEITED
K. HEMORRHAGE
L. FRONT
M. PORTER
N. STRAINED
O. COMMENCED
P. GROGGY

1. Examining carefully
2. Having a very high opinion of oneself
3. Not clear in meaning
4. Started
5. Weak or dizzy; not fully alert
6. Buses or trucks
7. Tight band used to stop bleeding
8. Strong feeling of guilt or sorrow
9. One who is hired to carry baggage
10. Bullet; shell
11. The leading position in a war
12. Very religious
13. Reduce someone's confidence
14. Bleeding; a loss of blood
15. Put in prison
16. Full of tension; nervous

A=	B=	C=	D=
E=	F=	G=	H=
I=	J=	K=	L=
M=	N=	O=	P=

A Farewell To Arms Vocabulary Magic Squares 1 Answer Key

A. DEVOUT
B. PUNCTURE
C. SCRUTINIZING
D. REMORSE
E. CAMIONS
F. VAGUE
G. INTERN
H. PROJECTILE
I. TOURNIQUET
J. CONCEITED
K. HEMORRHAGE
L. FRONT
M. PORTER
N. STRAINED
O. COMMENCED
P. GROGGY

1. Examining carefully
2. Having a very high opinion of oneself
3. Not clear in meaning
4. Started
5. Weak or dizzy; not fully alert
6. Buses or trucks
7. Tight band used to stop bleeding
8. Strong feeling of guilt or sorrow
9. One who is hired to carry baggage
10. Bullet; shell
11. The leading position in a war
12. Very religious
13. Reduce someone's confidence
14. Bleeding; a loss of blood
15. Put in prison
16. Full of tension; nervous

A=12	B=13	C=1	D=8
E=6	F=3	G=15	H=10
I=7	J=2	K=14	L=11
M=9	N=16	O=4	P=5

A Farewell To Arms Vocabulary Magic Squares 2

A. DECORATED
B. EMERY
C. AGITATORS
D. DRESSING
E. DORMER
F. OFFENSIVE
G. SECTOR
H. IMPARTIALLY
I. ARTICULATION
J. ELATED
K. DISMAL
L. FALLACY
M. TRUSS
N. RUPTURE
O. BATTERY
P. REGIMENT

1. A tear in tissue in the body; a hernia
2. Zone; division
3. Belief that is actually incorrect
4. Given a medal or other honor
5. Gloomy; depressing
6. Sandpaper
7. Medical device used to support a hernia
8. Fairly
9. Window built at right angles to the roof
10. A grouping of military troops
11. Protesters; troublemakers
12. Happy and excited
13. Bandages & things pertaining to treating wounds
14. Connection; fitting together
15. An attack or assault
16. Unit of guns or other weapons

A=	B=	C=	D=
E=	F=	G=	H=
I=	J=	K=	L=
M=	N=	O=	P=

A Farewell To Arms Vocabulary Magic Squares 2 Answer Key

A. DECORATED
B. EMERY
C. AGITATORS
D. DRESSING
E. DORMER
F. OFFENSIVE
G. SECTOR
H. IMPARTIALLY
I. ARTICULATION
J. ELATED
K. DISMAL
L. FALLACY
M. TRUSS
N. RUPTURE
O. BATTERY
P. REGIMENT

1. A tear in tissue in the body; a hernia
2. Zone; division
3. Belief that is actually incorrect
4. Given a medal or other honor
5. Gloomy; depressing
6. Sandpaper
7. Medical device used to support a hernia
8. Fairly
9. Window built at right angles to the roof
10. A grouping of military troops
11. Protesters; troublemakers
12. Happy and excited
13. Bandages & things pertaining to treating wounds
14. Connection; fitting together
15. An attack or assault
16. Unit of guns or other weapons

A=4	B=6	C=11	D=13
E=9	F=15	G=2	H=8
I=14	J=12	K=5	L=3
M=7	N=1	O=16	P=10

A Farewell To Arms Vocabulary Magic Squares 3

A. EVACUATES
B. HOSTILE
C. DECORATED
D. HEMORRHAGE
E. FRAGMENTS
F. CONCEITED
G. SENTIMENT
H. RUPTURE
I. SOLEMN
J. BILE
K. CAMIONS
L. PROTRACTED
M. FRONT
N. SECTOR
O. COAGULATES
P. INVIGORATING

1. Having a very high opinion of oneself
2. Serious; humorless
3. Thickens; clots; sticks together
4. Bleeding; a loss of blood
5. The leading position in a war
6. Unfriendly; showing hatred toward another
7. A tear in tissue in the body; a hernia
8. Buses or trucks
9. Given a medal or other honor
10. Filling with energy
11. Fluid produced in the liver
12. Small pieces of something shattered
13. Lasting for a long time
14. Thoughts based on feelings
15. Leaves a dangerous place
16. Zone; division

A=	B=	C=	D=
E=	F=	G=	H=
I=	J=	K=	L=
M=	N=	O=	P=

A Farewell To Arms Vocabulary Magic Squares 3 Answer Key

A. EVACUATES
B. HOSTILE
C. DECORATED
D. HEMORRHAGE
E. FRAGMENTS
F. CONCEITED
G. SENTIMENT
H. RUPTURE
I. SOLEMN
J. BILE
K. CAMIONS
L. PROTRACTED
M. FRONT
N. SECTOR
O. COAGULATES
P. INVIGORATING

1. Having a very high opinion of oneself
2. Serious; humorless
3. Thickens; clots; sticks together
4. Bleeding; a loss of blood
5. The leading position in a war
6. Unfriendly; showing hatred toward another
7. A tear in tissue in the body; a hernia
8. Buses or trucks
9. Given a medal or other honor
10. Filling with energy
11. Fluid produced in the liver
12. Small pieces of something shattered
13. Lasting for a long time
14. Thoughts based on feelings
15. Leaves a dangerous place
16. Zone; division

A=15	B=6	C=9	D=4
E=12	F=1	G=14	H=7
I=2	J=11	K=8	L=13
M=5	N=16	O=3	P=10

A Farewell To Arms Vocabulary Magic Squares 4

A. ARTILLERY
B. EMERY
C. GROGGY
D. VAGUE
E. TOURNIQUET
F. DOMINEERING
G. REMORSE
H. ATHEISTS
I. GYPS
J. FORMALITIES
K. SQUABBLED
L. TRUSS
M. EXALTED
N. EVACUATES
O. FRONT
P. ELATED

1. The leading position in a war
2. Not clear in meaning
3. Official procedures that must be followed
4. Tight band used to stop bleeding
5. Cheats out of money
6. Bossy or controlling
7. Happy and excited
8. Weak or dizzy; not fully alert
9. People who do not believe in God
10. Argued
11. Large guns and cannons
12. Leaves a dangerous place
13. Sandpaper
14. Praiseworthy
15. Strong feeling of guilt or sorrow
16. Medical device used to support a hernia

A=	B=	C=	D=
E=	F=	G=	H=
I=	J=	K=	L=
M=	N=	O=	P=

A Farewell To Arms Vocabulary Magic Squares 4 Answer Key

A. ARTILLERY
B. EMERY
C. GROGGY
D. VAGUE
E. TOURNIQUET
F. DOMINEERING
G. REMORSE
H. ATHEISTS
I. GYPS
J. FORMALITIES
K. SQUABBLED
L. TRUSS
M. EXALTED
N. EVACUATES
O. FRONT
P. ELATED

1. The leading position in a war
2. Not clear in meaning
3. Official procedures that must be followed
4. Tight band used to stop bleeding
5. Cheats out of money
6. Bossy or controlling
7. Happy and excited
8. Weak or dizzy; not fully alert
9. People who do not believe in God
10. Argued
11. Large guns and cannons
12. Leaves a dangerous place
13. Sandpaper
14. Praiseworthy
15. Strong feeling of guilt or sorrow
16. Medical device used to support a hernia

A=11	B=13	C=8	D=2
E=4	F=6	G=15	H=9
I=5	J=3	K=10	L=16
M=14	N=12	O=1	P=7

A Farewell To Arms Vocabulary Word Search 1

```
T O U R N I Q U E T S T R A I N E D T S
R B H U D I S M A L D D R E S S I N G D
U I V C E I Y D I S N O I M A C E D Y R
S L C K V N C O M S C A R C E R H R E M
S E H S O F A M P T O J L M R V E M T S
H R T A U A L I A P A B V O E T O N I X
M U E C T N L N R C G S T W T R E I N D
H T L K N T A E T O U C C A S M W N T Z
G P I H M R F E I N L H B E I G Q V E L
F U T B E Y R R A C A A W T Y R D I R B
B R S L L B O I L E T L N H R O F G N C
S P O T O B L N L I E E R T E G P O O X
Z H H N S P Y G Y T S T N E M G A R F D
C T E C T U N X U E T E G K E Y D A Y R
F L E D J N D A J D M D C B N I W T V L
R N H G S C T N H I I D E T A L E I A W
E E X A L T E D G R H J R L O M H N G J
B S L J G U D E L B B A U Q S R P G U G
P O R T E R R A R T I L L E R Y Q F E R
S W O L L E B A N A R C H I S T D Y D L
```

A disease of the intestines caused by bacteria (7)
A grouping of military troops (8)
A tear in tissue in the body; a hernia (7)
Argued (9)
Backpack (8)
Bandages & things pertaining to treating wounds (8)
Belief that is actually incorrect (7)
Bossy or controlling (11)
Buses or trucks (7)
Causes water to flow or drop off (5)
Cheats out of money (4)
Fairly (11)
Fast, powerful flood of water (7)
Filling with energy (12)
Fluid produced in the liver (4)
Force apart or open with a lever (3)
Full of tension; nervous (8)
Gloomy; depressing (6)
Happy and excited (6)
Having a very high opinion of oneself (9)
In short or limited supply (6)
Large guns and cannons (9)
Long, narrow hilltop (5)
Medical device used to support a hernia (5)
Morally offensive (7)
Not clear in meaning (5)
One who is hired to carry baggage (6)
One who thinks government should be abandoned (9)
Pleasant; friendly (7)
Praiseworthy (7)
Put in prison (6)
Reduce someone's confidence (8)
Sandpaper (5)
Serious; humorless (6)
Shouts in a loud, deep voice (7)
Small pieces of something shattered (9)
Soldiers who fight on foot (8)
Strong feeling of guilt or sorrow (7)
Sudden, violent bursts of wind (5)
Tense; tight (4)
The leading position in a war (5)
Thickens; clots; sticks together (10)
Thoughts based on feelings (9)
Tight band used to stop bleeding (10)
Traditional Swiss wooden cottage (6)
Unfriendly; showing hatred toward another (7)
Unit of guns or other weapons (7)
Very religious (6)
Weak or dizzy; not fully alert (6)
Window built at right angles to the roof (6)
Zone; division (6)

A Farewell To Arms Vocabulary Word Search 1 Answer Key

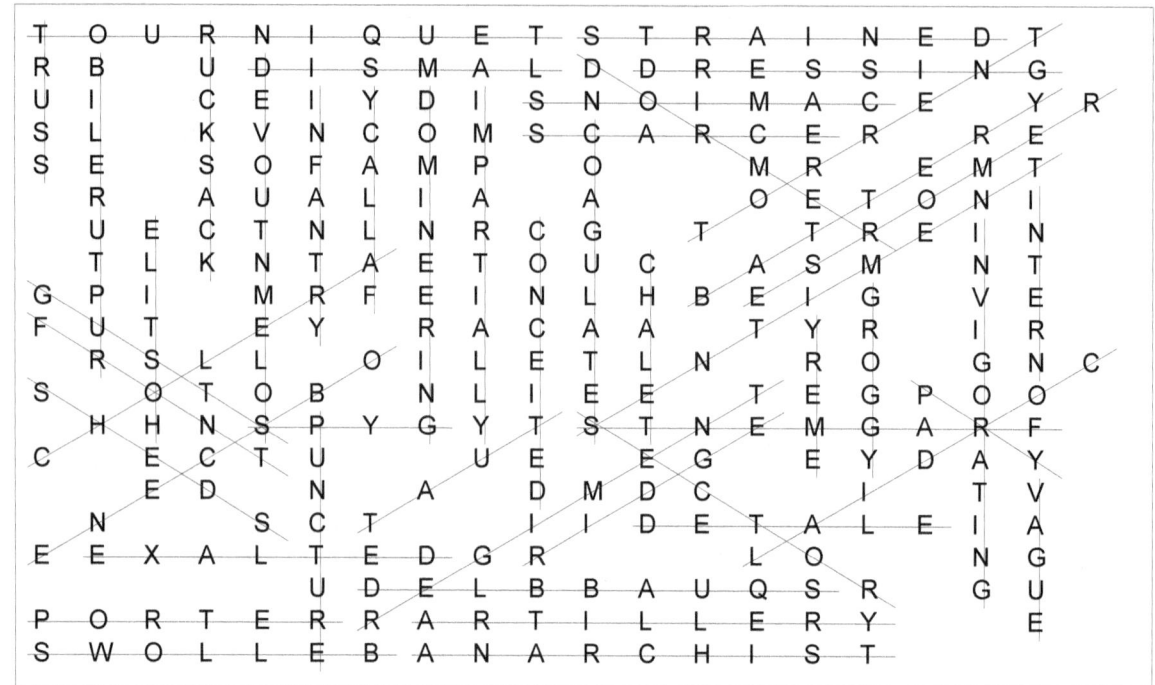

A disease of the intestines caused by bacteria (7)
A grouping of military troops (8)
A tear in tissue in the body; a hernia (7)
Argued (9)
Backpack (8)
Bandages & things pertaining to treating wounds (8)
Belief that is actually incorrect (7)
Bossy or controlling (11)
Buses or trucks (7)
Causes water to flow or drop off (5)
Cheats out of money (4)
Fairly (11)
Fast, powerful flood of water (7)
Filling with energy (12)
Fluid produced in the liver (4)
Force apart or open with a lever (3)
Full of tension; nervous (8)
Gloomy; depressing (6)
Happy and excited (6)
Having a very high opinion of oneself (9)
In short or limited supply (6)
Large guns and cannons (9)
Long, narrow hilltop (5)
Medical device used to support a hernia (5)
Morally offensive (7)
Not clear in meaning (5)

One who is hired to carry baggage (6)
One who thinks government should be abandoned (9)
Pleasant; friendly (7)
Praiseworthy (7)
Put in prison (6)
Reduce someone's confidence (8)
Sandpaper (5)
Serious; humorless (6)
Shouts in a loud, deep voice (7)
Small pieces of something shattered (9)
Soldiers who fight on foot (8)
Strong feeling of guilt or sorrow (7)
Sudden, violent bursts of wind (5)
Tense; tight (4)
The leading position in a war (5)
Thickens; clots; sticks together (10)
Thoughts based on feelings (9)
Tight band used to stop bleeding (10)
Traditional Swiss wooden cottage (6)
Unfriendly; showing hatred toward another (7)
Unit of guns or other weapons (7)
Very religious (6)
Weak or dizzy; not fully alert (6)
Window built at right angles to the roof (6)
Zone; division (6)

A Farewell To Arms Vocabulary Word Search 2

```
O T L N O I T A L U C I T R A X F B W Y
B C O A G U L A T E S Y H S N O I M A C
S H O S T I L E U S S S N E Z D E T S D
T A N A R C H I S T O N U I S A N C E S
A S W O L L E B U S L K F T C Q E D T Y
C T K X A B W O W I E C M I C I C X A L
L R F M Q N V R F L M A H L H I S N U Z
E A S L J E T I R A N S R A O N B M C F
S I I I E D Y N D O I G K U M L T O A A K
D N E I N S E G N C D C P R E E S I V S
E E D N N T M E T O H U T O R R T R E M
T D S F L S I C R S C R U F A N N O U C
I Y S A X U G M E H U Q R T E D E N G F
E R X N P G E S E S W J E R E Z M L A P
C E Z T W R R E S N P O R T E R G Y V D
N T R R X O Y C D J T O A L T M A Y T M
O T Y Y M H V T W X T L Y G G O R G P C
C A L E L I B O D Q E C R A C S F X R S
J B R D E N O R E P A H C N U N V G V D
A G I T A T O R S E M E R Y C A L L A F
```

A disease of the intestines caused by bacteria (7)
A grouping of military troops (8)
A tear in tissue in the body; a hernia (7)
Annoyance; irritation (8)
Backpack (8)
Belief that is actually incorrect (7)
Buses or trucks (7)
Causes water to flow or drop off (5)
Cheats out of money (4)
Connection; fitting together (12)
Fast, powerful flood of water (7)
Fluid produced in the liver (4)
Force apart or open with a lever (3)
Full of tension; nervous (8)
Gloomy; depressing (6)
Happy and excited (6)
Having a very high opinion of oneself (9)
In short or limited supply (6)
Leaves a dangerous place (9)
Like a mature woman with sensible qualities (8)
Long, narrow hilltop (5)
Medical device used to support a hernia (5)
Morally offensive (7)
Negative sarcasm or mockery (8)
Not accompanied by a supervisor (12)
Not clear in meaning (5)
Official procedures that must be followed (11)
One who is hired to carry baggage (6)
One who thinks government should be abandoned (9)
People who believe in control by the people (10)
Praiseworthy (7)
Protesters; troublemakers (9)
Put in prison (6)
Sandpaper (5)
Serious; humorless (6)
Shouts in a loud, deep voice (7)
Small pieces of something shattered (9)
Soldiers who fight on foot (8)
Strong feeling of guilt or sorrow (7)
Sudden, violent bursts of wind (5)
Tense; tight (4)
The leading position in a war (5)
Thickens; clots; sticks together (10)
Things that get in the way or stop progress (9)
Thoughts based on feelings (9)
Traditional Swiss wooden cottage (6)
Unfriendly; showing hatred toward another (7)
Unit of guns or other weapons (7)
Very religious (6)
Weak or dizzy; not fully alert (6)
Window built at right angles to the roof (6)
Zone; division (6)

A Farewell To Arms Vocabulary Word Search 2 Answer Key

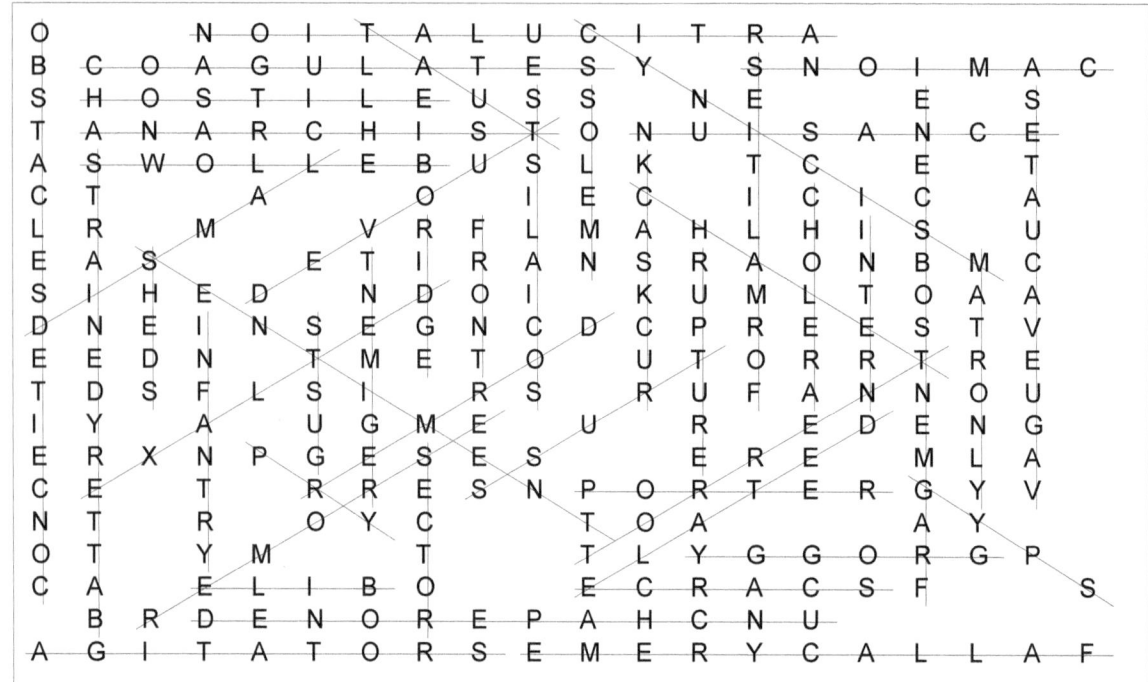

A disease of the intestines caused by bacteria (7)
A grouping of military troops (8)
A tear in tissue in the body; a hernia (7)
Annoyance; irritation (8)
Backpack (8)
Belief that is actually incorrect (7)
Buses or trucks (7)
Causes water to flow or drop off (5)
Cheats out of money (4)
Connection; fitting together (12)
Fast, powerful flood of water (7)
Fluid produced in the liver (4)
Force apart or open with a lever (3)
Full of tension; nervous (8)
Gloomy; depressing (6)
Happy and excited (6)
Having a very high opinion of oneself (9)
In short or limited supply (6)
Leaves a dangerous place (9)
Like a mature woman with sensible qualities (8)
Long, narrow hilltop (5)
Medical device used to support a hernia (5)
Morally offensive (7)
Negative sarcasm or mockery (8)
Not accompanied by a supervisor (12)
Not clear in meaning (5)
Official procedures that must be followed (11)

One who is hired to carry baggage (6)
One who thinks government should be abandoned (9)
People who believe in control by the people (10)
Praiseworthy (7)
Protesters; troublemakers (9)
Put in prison (6)
Sandpaper (5)
Serious; humorless (6)
Shouts in a loud, deep voice (7)
Small pieces of something shattered (9)
Soldiers who fight on foot (8)
Strong feeling of guilt or sorrow (7)
Sudden, violent bursts of wind (5)
Tense; tight (4)
The leading position in a war (5)
Thickens; clots; sticks together (10)
Things that get in the way or stop progress (9)
Thoughts based on feelings (9)
Traditional Swiss wooden cottage (6)
Unfriendly; showing hatred toward another (7)
Unit of guns or other weapons (7)
Very religious (6)
Weak or dizzy; not fully alert (6)
Window built at right angles to the roof (6)
Zone; division (6)

A Farewell To Arms Vocabulary Word Search 3

```
S O C I A L I S T S E X A L T E D S B R
X Z M O G T S N O I M A C O Y C N W P S
T K S N N W H G T M D Q N C B M F O P T
I A B T I C K E S E Z R A Q C S G L Q R
B N U G R Y E I I P R L Y T G C C L S A
S I F T E L C I S S L N N S F A C E Q I
E B L A E I P O T A T O N S E R L B N N
N C D E N I A R F E R S P U N C T U R E
T B G Y I T L T O F D G G R A E P N L D
I R C M R R Z R B E A Y T Y D M I F N
M I F E O U U Y M A V N S P O R T E R F
E T R G D C N S A T J B S R S C I U R C
N T A I M K G Q L T O E M I E G P D P Y
T L G M A S A U I E C E C J V T P I G G
U E M E T A I A T R R H O T U E R S E E
O N E N R C N B I Y Y R O R O O Y M L S
V E N T O K L B E L P J E L T R X A A K
E S T J N S Y L S H E D S C E L Y L T F
D S S V L N M E L O S D E C O R A T E D
Q T P Y Y M V D R E S S I N G M A Q D Y
H E M O R R H A G E V A C U A T E S M Y
G U S T S A R T I C U L A T I O N Y M V
```

ARTICULATION	DEVOUT	FRAGMENTS	PORTER	SENTIMENT
ATHEISTS	DISMAL	FRONT	PROJECTILE	SHEDS
BATTERY	DOMINEERING	GUSTS	PRY	SOCIALISTS
BELLOWS	DORMER	GYPS	PUNCTURE	SOLEMN
BILE	DRESSING	HEMORRHAGE	REFRAINED	SQUABBLED
BRITTLENESS	ELATED	INFANTRY	REGIMENT	STRAINED
CAMIONS	EMERY	INTERN	RIDGE	TAUT
CHOLERA	EVACUATES	MATRONLY	RUCKSACK	TRAJECTORY
CONCEITED	EXALTED	OBSCENE	RUPTURE	TRUSS
CYNICISM	FALLACY	OBSTACLES	SCARCE	UNGAINLY
DECORATED	FORMALITIES	OFFENSIVE	SECTOR	VAGUE

A Farewell To Arms Vocabulary Word Search 3 Answer Key

ARTICULATION	DEVOUT	FRAGMENTS	PORTER	SENTIMENT
ATHEISTS	DISMAL	FRONT	PROJECTILE	SHEDS
BATTERY	DOMINEERING	GUSTS	PRY	SOCIALISTS
BELLOWS	DORMER	GYPS	PUNCTURE	SOLEMN
BILE	DRESSING	HEMORRHAGE	REFRAINED	SQUABBLED
BRITTLENESS	ELATED	INFANTRY	REGIMENT	STRAINED
CAMIONS	EMERY	INTERN	RIDGE	TAUT
CHOLERA	EVACUATES	MATRONLY	RUCKSACK	TRAJECTORY
CONCEITED	EXALTED	OBSCENE	RUPTURE	TRUSS
CYNICISM	FALLACY	OBSTACLES	SCARCE	UNGAINLY
DECORATED	FORMALITIES	OFFENSIVE	SECTOR	VAGUE

A Farewell To Arms Vocabulary Word Search 4

```
S H E D S Z H P Z S P O R T E R K Z S Y
O D P U N C T U R E E E S T N E R R O T
C Y N I C I S M V Y C N D I S M A L Y O
I C D D O R M E R R S C T C N O Y D B C
A R A J R E E F A A E B O I D R T S H X
L P S M D L M C R K I G V M M S C A D Y
I E G D I R S E L A T E D N M E L O S D
S Q C T A O L Z R F I E E C N E N P P J
T D S J L O N P W Y L T C E T N N T Y R
S O G B H B R S W B A T O D T Y S C G M
H B Y C W I W J B G M D R Y R G R N E P
L S M V F L M A F B R V A E A G O R L D
E T S A P E U R S E O S T P J O T E D D
G A E G Y Q U T S M F T E R E R A T E V
I C C U S P S S C Q A N D O C G T N V S
T L T E T I I I E B L E M J T Q I I O Q
I E O U E N T H X E L M W E O A G T U F
M S R H G A W C A L A G P C R T A U T F
A E T V T S P R L L C A W T Y F R O N T
T A W I K P D A T O Y R S I G U S T S Y
E R O N F L T N E W Q F Y L N O R T A M
X N B L F Q M A D S S D G E T R U S S D
```

AGITATORS	CORDIAL	FORMALITIES	OBSTACLES	SHEDS
ANARCHIST	CYNICISM	FRAGMENTS	PORTER	SOCIALISTS
ATHEISTS	DECORATED	FRONT	PROJECTILE	SOLEMN
BATTERY	DEVOUT	GROGGY	PRY	SQUABBLED
BELLOWS	DISMAL	GUSTS	PUNCTURE	STRAINED
BILE	DORMER	GYPS	REMORSE	TAUT
CAMIONS	DRESSING	HOSTILE	RIDGE	TORRENT
CHALET	ELATED	INTERN	RUPTURE	TRAJECTORY
CHOLERA	EMERY	LEGITIMATE	SCARCE	TRUSS
CITATION	EXALTED	MATRONLY	SECTOR	VAGUE
COMMENCED	FALLACY	OBSCENE	SENTIMENT	

A Farewell To Arms Vocabulary Word Search 4 Answer Key

AGITATORS	CORDIAL	FORMALITIES	OBSTACLES	SHEDS
ANARCHIST	CYNICISM	FRAGMENTS	PORTER	SOCIALISTS
ATHEISTS	DECORATED	FRONT	PROJECTILE	SOLEMN
BATTERY	DEVOUT	GROGGY	PRY	SQUABBLED
BELLOWS	DISMAL	GUSTS	PUNCTURE	STRAINED
BILE	DORMER	GYPS	REMORSE	TAUT
CAMIONS	DRESSING	HOSTILE	RIDGE	TORRENT
CHALET	ELATED	INTERN	RUPTURE	TRAJECTORY
CHOLERA	EMERY	LEGITIMATE	SCARCE	TRUSS
CITATION	EXALTED	MATRONLY	SECTOR	VAGUE
COMMENCED	FALLACY	OBSCENE	SENTIMENT	

A Farewell To Arms Vocabulary Crossword 1

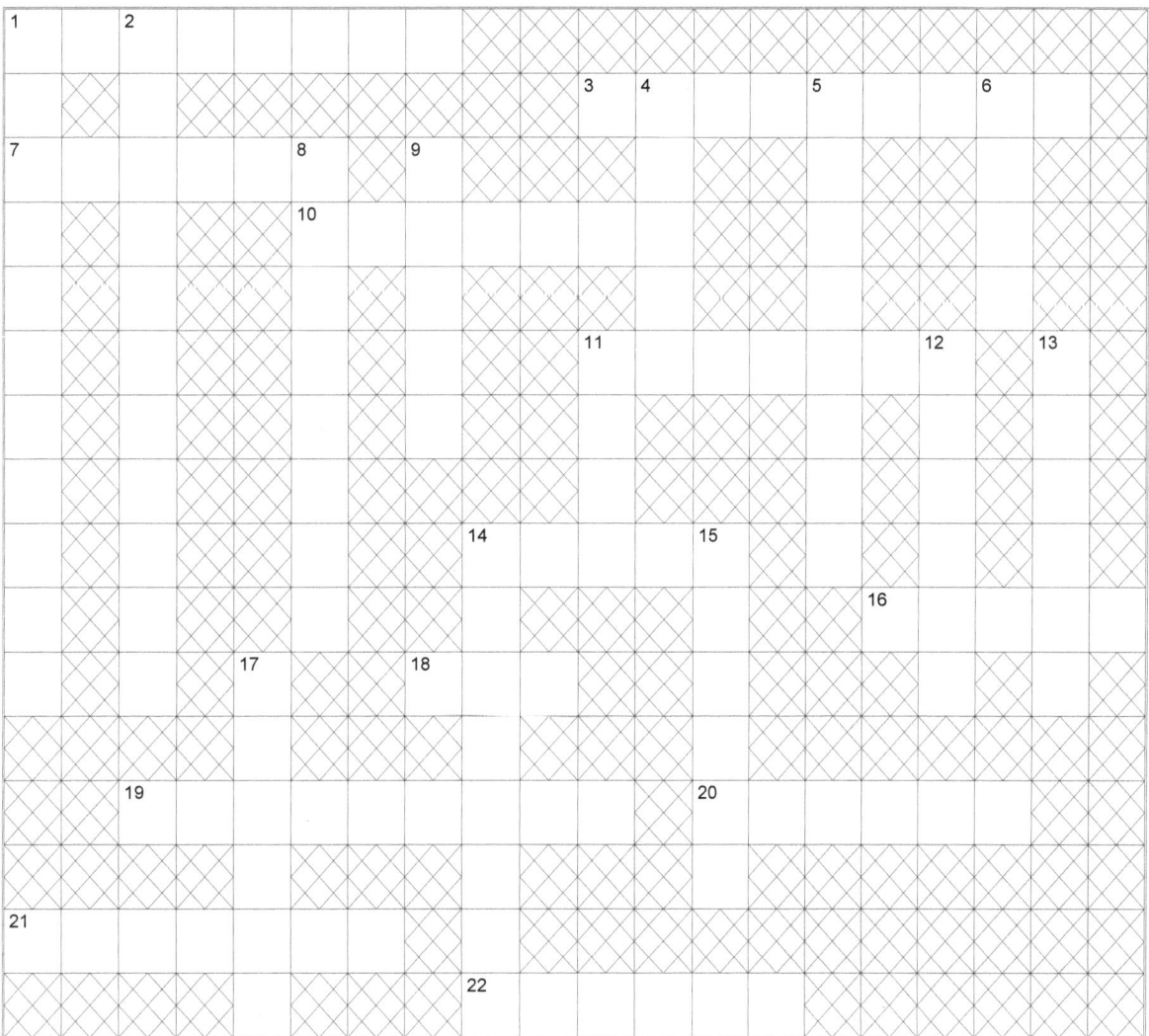

Across
1. Soldiers who fight on foot
3. Small pieces of something shattered
7. One who is hired to carry baggage
10. Praiseworthy
11. Shouts in a loud, deep voice
14. Causes water to flow or drop off
16. Sandpaper
18. Force apart or open with a lever
19. One who thinks government should be abandoned
20. Traditional Swiss wooden cottage
21. Fast, powerful flood of water
22. Very religious

Down
1. Fairly
2. Official procedures that must be followed
4. Long, narrow hilltop
5. Like a mature woman with sensible qualities
6. Tense; tight
8. A grouping of military troops
9. Not clear in meaning
11. Fluid produced in the liver
12. Serious; humorless
13. Put in prison
14. Full of tension; nervous
15. In short or limited supply
17. Happy and excited

A Farewell To Arms Vocabulary Crossword 1 Answer Key

	1 I	N	2 F	A	N	T	R	Y							
	M		O						3 F	4 R	A	5 G	M	6 E	N	T	S
	7 P	O	R	T	E	8 R		9 V		I		A		A
	A		M			10 E	X	A	L	T	E	D		U
	R		A			G		G		G		R		T
	T		L			I		U		11 B	E	L	L	O	W	12 S		13 I
	I		I			M		E		I				N		O		N
	A		T			E								L		L		T
	L		I			N		14 S	H	E	D	15 S		Y		E		E
	L		E			T		T				C			16 E	M	E	R	Y
	Y		S	17 E		18 P	R	Y				A				N		N
				L				A				R						
			19 A	N	A	R	C	H	I	S	T	20 C	H	A	L	E	T
				T				N				E					
	21 T	O	R	R	E	N	T	E									
				D				22 D	E	V	O	U	T				

Across
1. Soldiers who fight on foot
3. Small pieces of something shattered
7. One who is hired to carry baggage
10. Praiseworthy
11. Shouts in a loud, deep voice
14. Causes water to flow or drop off
16. Sandpaper
18. Force apart or open with a lever
19. One who thinks government should be abandoned
20. Traditional Swiss wooden cottage
21. Fast, powerful flood of water
22. Very religious

Down
1. Fairly
2. Official procedures that must be followed
4. Long, narrow hilltop
5. Like a mature woman with sensible qualities
6. Tense; tight
8. A grouping of military troops
9. Not clear in meaning
11. Fluid produced in the liver
12. Serious; humorless
13. Put in prison
14. Full of tension; nervous
15. In short or limited supply
17. Happy and excited

A Farewell To Arms Vocabulary Crossword 2

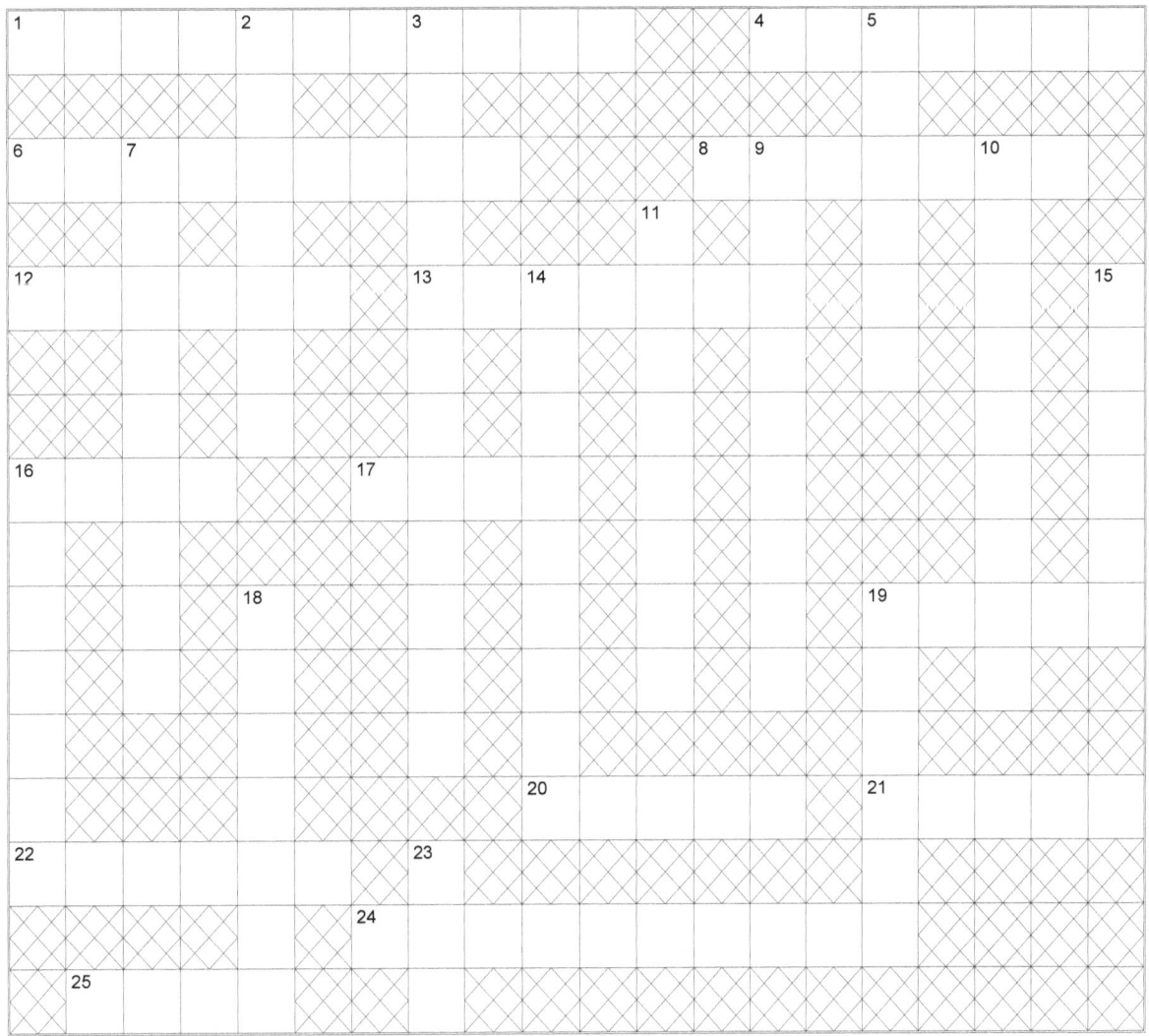

Across
1. Fairly
4. Unfriendly; showing hatred toward another
6. Small pieces of something shattered
8. Belief that is actually incorrect
12. Put in prison
13. A disease of the intestines caused by bacteria
16. Fluid produced in the liver
17. Tense; tight
19. Sandpaper
20. Causes water to flow or drop off
21. Medical device used to support a hernia
22. Zone; division
24. Lasting for a long time
25. Cheats out of money

Down
2. Strong feeling of guilt or sorrow
3. Connection; fitting together
5. Serious; humorless
7. Large guns and cannons
9. One who thinks government should be abandoned
10. Started
11. A grouping of military troops
14. Things that get in the way or stop progress
15. Weak or dizzy; not fully alert
16. Shouts in a loud, deep voice
18. Buses or trucks
19. Happy and excited
23. Force apart or open with a lever

A Farewell To Arms Vocabulary Crossword 2 Answer Key

	1 I	M	2 P	A	R	T	I	A	L	L	Y		4 H	5 O	S	T	I	L	E
				E		R								O					
6 F	R	7 A	G	M	E	N	T	S			8 F	9 A	L	L	A	10 C	Y		
		R		O		I				11 R		N		E		O			
12 I	N	T	E	R	N		13 C	14 H	O	L	E	R	A		M		M		15 G
		I		S			U		B		G		R		N		M		R
		L		E			L		S		I		C				E		O
16 B	I	L	E			17 T	A	U	T		M		H				N		G
E		E					T		A		E		I				C		G
L		R		18 C			I		C		N		S		19 E	M	E	R	Y
L		Y		A			O		L		T		T		L		D		
O				M			N		E						A				
W				I					20 S	H	E	D	S		21 T	R	U	S	S
22 S	E	C	T	O	R		23 P								E				
				N		24 P	R	O	T	R	A	C	T	E	D				
		25 G	Y	P	S		Y												

Across
1. Fairly
4. Unfriendly; showing hatred toward another
6. Small pieces of something shattered
8. Belief that is actually incorrect
12. Put in prison
13. A disease of the intestines caused by bacteria
16. Fluid produced in the liver
17. Tense; tight
19. Sandpaper
20. Causes water to flow or drop off
21. Medical device used to support a hernia
22. Zone; division
24. Lasting for a long time
25. Cheats out of money

Down
2. Strong feeling of guilt or sorrow
3. Connection; fitting together
5. Serious; humorless
7. Large guns and cannons
9. One who thinks government should be abandoned
10. Started
11. A grouping of military troops
14. Things that get in the way or stop progress
15. Weak or dizzy; not fully alert
16. Shouts in a loud, deep voice
18. Buses or trucks
19. Happy and excited
23. Force apart or open with a lever

A Farewell To Arms Vocabulary Crossword 3

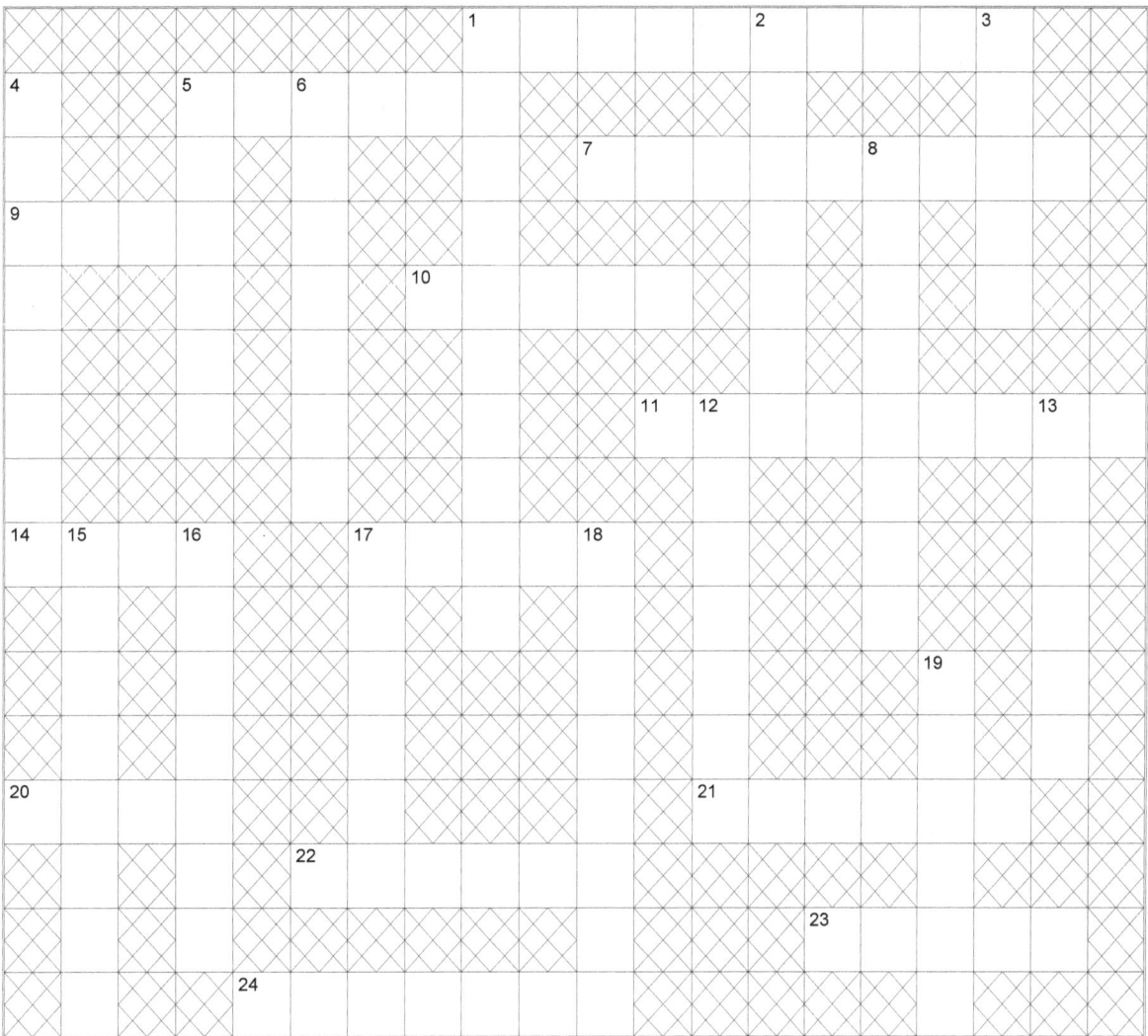

Across
1. Bullet; shell
5. Window built at right angles to the roof
7. Started
9. Cheats out of money
10. The leading position in a war
11. Things that get in the way or stop progress
14. Tense; tight
17. Causes water to flow or drop off
20. Fluid produced in the liver
21. Zone; division
22. Put in prison
23. Not clear in meaning
24. Praiseworthy

Down
1. Lasting for a long time
2. Buses or trucks
3. Sandpaper
4. A grouping of military troops
5. Gloomy; depressing
6. Strong feeling of guilt or sorrow
8. Annoyance; irritation
12. Shouts in a loud, deep voice
13. Happy and excited
15. People who do not believe in God
16. Fast, powerful flood of water
17. Serious; humorless
18. Full of tension; nervous
19. Weak or dizzy; not fully alert

A Farewell To Arms Vocabulary Crossword 3 Answer Key

							¹P	R	O	J	E	²C	T	¹I	L	³E	
⁴R		⁵D	O	⁶R	M	E	R					A				M	
E		I		E			O		⁷C	O	M	M	E	⁸N	C	E	D
⁹G	Y	P	S	M			T		I			U		R			
I		M		O		¹⁰F	R	O	N	T		O		I		Y	
M		A		R		A						N		S			
E		L		S		C			¹¹O	¹²B	S	T	A	C	L	¹³E	S
N				E		T				E				N		L	
¹⁴T	¹⁵A	¹⁶U		¹⁷S	H	E	D	¹⁸S		L				C		A	
	T	O		O		D		T		L				E		T	
	H	R		L				R		O				¹⁹G		E	
	E	R		E				A		W				R		D	
²⁰B	I	L	E			M		I		²¹S	E	C	T	O	R		
	S		N		²²I	N	T	E	R	N				G			
	T		T					E				²³V	A	G	U	E	
	S		²⁴E	X	A	L	T	E	D					Y			

Across
1. Bullet; shell
5. Window built at right angles to the roof
7. Started
9. Cheats out of money
10. The leading position in a war
11. Things that get in the way or stop progress
14. Tense; tight
17. Causes water to flow or drop off
20. Fluid produced in the liver
21. Zone; division
22. Put in prison
23. Not clear in meaning
24. Praiseworthy

Down
1. Lasting for a long time
2. Buses or trucks
3. Sandpaper
4. A grouping of military troops
5. Gloomy; depressing
6. Strong feeling of guilt or sorrow
8. Annoyance; irritation
12. Shouts in a loud, deep voice
13. Happy and excited
15. People who do not believe in God
16. Fast, powerful flood of water
17. Serious; humorless
18. Full of tension; nervous
19. Weak or dizzy; not fully alert

A Farewell To Arms Vocabulary Crossword 4

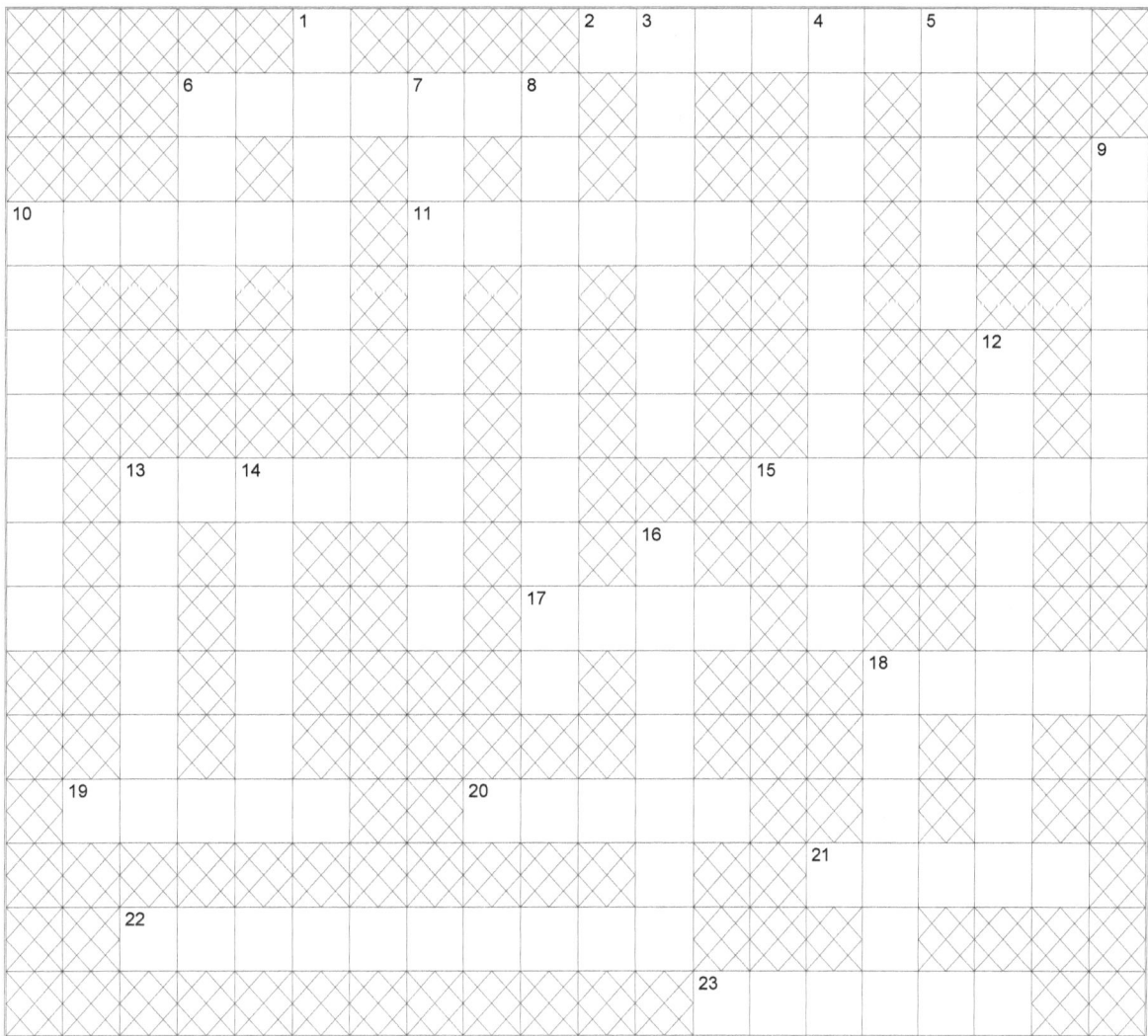

Across
2. Large guns and cannons
6. Shouts in a loud, deep voice
10. Traditional Swiss wooden cottage
11. Zone; division
13. Gloomy; depressing
15. Belief that is actually incorrect
17. Tense; tight
18. Causes water to flow or drop off
19. The leading position in a war
20. Not clear in meaning
21. Medical device used to support a hernia
22. Bullet; shell
23. Put in prison

Down
1. Happy and excited
3. Strong feeling of guilt or sorrow
4. Legal; lawful
5. Sandpaper
6. Fluid produced in the liver
7. Things that get in the way or stop progress
8. People who believe in control by the people
9. Weak or dizzy; not fully alert
10. A disease of the intestines caused by bacteria
12. Small pieces of something shattered
13. Window built at right angles to the roof
14. Serious; humorless
16. A tear in tissue in the body; a hernia
18. In short or limited supply

A Farewell To Arms Vocabulary Crossword 4 Answer Key

Across
2. Large guns and cannons
6. Shouts in a loud, deep voice
10. Traditional Swiss wooden cottage
11. Zone; division
13. Gloomy; depressing
15. Belief that is actually incorrect
17. Tense; tight
18. Causes water to flow or drop off
19. The leading position in a war
20. Not clear in meaning
21. Medical device used to support a hernia
22. Bullet; shell
23. Put in prison

Down
1. Happy and excited
3. Strong feeling of guilt or sorrow
4. Legal; lawful
5. Sandpaper
6. Fluid produced in the liver
7. Things that get in the way or stop progress
8. People who believe in control by the people
9. Weak or dizzy; not fully alert
10. A disease of the intestines caused by bacteria
12. Small pieces of something shattered
13. Window built at right angles to the roof
14. Serious; humorless
16. A tear in tissue in the body; a hernia
18. In short or limited supply

A Farewell To Arms Vocabulary Juggle Letters 1

1. CPEUTRUN = 1. _____
   Reduce someone's confidence

2. RILJEPOETC = 2. _____
   Bullet; shell

3. TETRORN = 3. _____
   Fast, powerful flood of water

4. NIDRFEAER = 4. _____
   Held back; kept from doing

5. ATYNNFIR = 5. _____
   Soldiers who fight on foot

6. OANISMC = 6. _____
   Buses or trucks

7. GPSY = 7. _____
   Cheats out of money

8. MTFAISILREO = 8. _____
   Official procedures that must be followed

9. OSEILTH = 9. _____
   Unfriendly; showing hatred toward another

10. ITISLSSAOC =10. _____
    People who believe in control by the people

11. SRSTU =11. _____
    Medical device used to support a hernia

12. REPRUUT =12. _____
    A tear in tissue in the body; a hernia

13. NHILIETORAAX =13. _____
    Happiness and excitement

14. SSEHD =14. _____
    Causes water to flow or drop off

15. SOELCBSTA =15. _____
    Things that get in the way or stop progress

A Farewell To Arms Vocabulary Juggle Letters 1 Answer Key

1. CPEUTRUN = 1. PUNCTURE
   Reduce someone's confidence

2. RILJEPOETC = 2. PROJECTILE
   Bullet; shell

3. TETRORN = 3. TORRENT
   Fast, powerful flood of water

4. NIDRFEAER = 4. REFRAINED
   Held back; kept from doing

5. ATYNNFIR = 5. INFANTRY
   Soldiers who fight on foot

6. OANISMC = 6. CAMIONS
   Buses or trucks

7. GPSY = 7. GYPS
   Cheats out of money

8. MTFAISILREO = 8. FORMALITIES
   Official procedures that must be followed

9. OSEILTH = 9. HOSTILE
   Unfriendly; showing hatred toward another

10. ITISLSSAOC =10. SOCIALISTS
    People who believe in control by the people

11. SRSTU =11. TRUSS
    Medical device used to support a hernia

12. REPRUUT =12. RUPTURE
    A tear in tissue in the body; a hernia

13. NHILIETORAAX =13. EXHILARATION
    Happiness and excitement

14. SSEHD =14. SHEDS
    Causes water to flow or drop off

15. SOELCBSTA =15. OBSTACLES
    Things that get in the way or stop progress

A Farewell To Arms Vocabulary Juggle Letters 2

1. NNIGAYLU = 1. _____
Clumsy; not graceful

2. SSRUT = 2. _____
Medical device used to support a hernia

3. TSAUVAEEC = 3. _____
Leaves a dangerous place

4. QEBUADBLS = 4. _____
Argued

5. LBWSOEL = 5. _____
Shouts in a loud, deep voice

6. AYOLTNMR = 6. _____
Like a mature woman with sensible qualities

7. XATEEDL = 7. _____
Praiseworthy

8. ASLIMD = 8. _____
Gloomy; depressing

9. RANYFITN = 9. _____
Soldiers who fight on foot

10. OEMNGIRNDEI =10. _____
Bossy or controlling

11. KCKSUCAR =11. _____
Backpack

12. PYR =12. _____
Force apart or open with a lever

13. NHEROPDACUEN =13. _____
Not accompanied by a supervisor

14. IDRGE =14. _____
Long, narrow hilltop

15. LYAALCF =15. _____
Belief that is actually incorrect

A Farewell To Arms Vocabulary Juggle Letters 2 Answer Key

1. NNIGAYLU = 1. UNGAINLY
   Clumsy; not graceful

2. SSRUT = 2. TRUSS
   Medical device used to support a hernia

3. TSAUVAEEC = 3. EVACUATES
   Leaves a dangerous place

4. QEBUADBLS = 4. SQUABBLED
   Argued

5. LBWSOEL = 5. BELLOWS
   Shouts in a loud, deep voice

6. AYOLTNMR = 6. MATRONLY
   Like a mature woman with sensible qualities

7. XATEEDL = 7. EXALTED
   Praiseworthy

8. ASLIMD = 8. DISMAL
   Gloomy; depressing

9. RANYFITN = 9. INFANTRY
   Soldiers who fight on foot

10. OEMNGIRNDEI =10. DOMINEERING
    Bossy or controlling

11. KCKSUCAR =11. RUCKSACK
    Backpack

12. PYR =12. PRY
    Force apart or open with a lever

13. NHEROPDACUEN =13. UNCHAPERONED
    Not accompanied by a supervisor

14. IDRGE =14. RIDGE
    Long, narrow hilltop

15. LYAALCF =15. FALLACY
    Belief that is actually incorrect

A Farewell To Arms Vocabulary Juggle Letters 3

1. ISITASCOLS = 1. _____
   People who believe in control by the people

2. NUUEIQTORT = 2. _____
   Tight band used to stop bleeding

3. RNTAIYFN = 3. _____
   Soldiers who fight on foot

4. NIMOASC = 4. _____
   Buses or trucks

5. TRTOYRAJEC = 5. _____
   Route; path

6. STRANCHIA = 6. _____
   One who thinks government should be abandoned

7. USGTS = 7. _____
   Sudden, violent bursts of wind

8. NTOITACI = 8. _____
   Official document of praise

9. UTNTSCYEUPOMOL = 9. _____
   In a disapproving way

10. EOCPRTRATD =10. _____
    Lasting for a long time

11. MEORRD =11. _____
    Window built at right angles to the roof

12. EEBCNSO =12. _____
    Morally offensive

13. ATNDSIER =13. _____
    Full of tension; nervous

14. UTAEEVSCA =14. _____
    Leaves a dangerous place

15. NDRSEIGS =15. _____
    Bandages & things pertaining to treating wounds

A Farewell To Arms Vocabulary Juggle Letters 3 Answer Key

1. ISITASCOLS = 1. SOCIALISTS
People who believe in control by the people

2. NUUEIQTORT = 2. TOURNIQUET
Tight band used to stop bleeding

3. RNTAIYFN = 3. INFANTRY
Soldiers who fight on foot

4. NIMOASC = 4. CAMIONS
Buses or trucks

5. TRTOYRAJEC = 5. TRAJECTORY
Route; path

6. STRANCHIA = 6. ANARCHIST
One who thinks government should be abandoned

7. USGTS = 7. GUSTS
Sudden, violent bursts of wind

8. NTOITACI = 8. CITATION
Official document of praise

9. UTNTSCYEUPOMOL = 9. CONTEMPTUOUSLY
In a disapproving way

10. EOCPRTRATD = 10. PROTRACTED
Lasting for a long time

11. MEORRD = 11. DORMER
Window built at right angles to the roof

12. EEBCNSO = 12. OBSCENE
Morally offensive

13. ATNDSIER = 13. STRAINED
Full of tension; nervous

14. UTAEEVSCA = 14. EVACUATES
Leaves a dangerous place

15. NDRSEIGS = 15. DRESSING
Bandages & things pertaining to treating wounds

A Farewell To Arms Vocabulary Juggle Letters 4

1. ALGTASECUO = 1. _____
   Thickens; clots; sticks together

2. MHHRGOREAE = 2. _____
   Bleeding; a loss of blood

3. NCUUPRTE = 3. _____
   Reduce someone's confidence

4. ITSEEMNNT = 4. _____
   Thoughts based on feelings

5. NSUCIEAN = 5. _____
   Annoyance; irritation

6. UTRERUP = 6. _____
   A tear in tissue in the body; a hernia

7. DETOEADCR = 7. _____
   Given a medal or other honor

8. ALIATMYPLIR = 8. _____
   Fairly

9. ORDLCAI = 9. _____
   Pleasant; friendly

10. LEETXDA = 10. _____
    Praiseworthy

11. IOSELTH = 11. _____
    Unfriendly; showing hatred toward another

12. OTEILMSIARF = 12. _____
    Official procedures that must be followed

13. ICTAOSISSL = 13. _____
    People who believe in control by the people

14. PYGS = 14. _____
    Cheats out of money

15. AMFSETNGR = 15. _____
    Small pieces of something shattered

A Farewell To Arms Vocabulary Juggle Letters 4 Answer Key

1. ALGTASECUO = 1. COAGULATES
   Thickens; clots; sticks together

2. MHHRGOREAE = 2. HEMORRHAGE
   Bleeding; a loss of blood

3. NCUUPRTE = 3. PUNCTURE
   Reduce someone's confidence

4. ITSEEMNNT = 4. SENTIMENT
   Thoughts based on feelings

5. NSUCIEAN = 5. NUISANCE
   Annoyance; irritation

6. UTRERUP = 6. RUPTURE
   A tear in tissue in the body; a hernia

7. DETOEADCR = 7. DECORATED
   Given a medal or other honor

8. ALIATMYPLIR = 8. IMPARTIALLY
   Fairly

9. ORDLCAI = 9. CORDIAL
   Pleasant; friendly

10. LEETXDA =10. EXALTED
    Praiseworthy

11. IOSELTH =11. HOSTILE
    Unfriendly; showing hatred toward another

12. OTEILMSIARF =12. FORMALITIES
    Official procedures that must be followed

13. ICTAOSISSL =13. SOCIALISTS
    People who believe in control by the people

14. PYGS =14. GYPS
    Cheats out of money

15. AMFSETNGR =15. FRAGMENTS
    Small pieces of something shattered

COMMENCED	Started
ARTILLERY	Large guns and cannons
CHOLERA	A disease of the intestines caused by bacteria
ATHEISTS	People who do not believe in God
BELLOWS	Shouts in a loud, deep voice

FRONT	The leading position in a war
BATTERY	Unit of guns or other weapons
OFFENSIVE	An attack or assault
RUPTURE	A tear in tissue in the body; a hernia
TRUSS	Medical device used to support a hernia

REGIMENT	A grouping of military troops
RIDGE	Long, narrow hilltop
DRESSING	Bandages & things pertaining to treating wounds
DECORATED	Given a medal or other honor
INFANTRY	Soldiers who fight on foot

CAMIONS	Buses or trucks
TOURNIQUET	Tight band used to stop bleeding
HEMORRHAGE	Bleeding; a loss of blood
COAGULATES	Thickens; clots; sticks together
FRAGMENTS	Small pieces of something shattered

PORTER	One who is hired to carry baggage
DOMINEERING	Bossy or controlling
SOLEMN	Serious; humorless
REFRAINED	Held back; kept from doing
SENTIMENT	Thoughts based on feelings

ARTICULATION	Connection; fitting together
CONSCIENTIOUSLY	Carefully; with thought; dutifully
PROJECTILE	Bullet; shell
EMERY	Sandpaper
FORMALITIES	Official procedures that must be followed

UNCHAPERONED	Not accompanied by a supervisor
CORDIAL	Pleasant; friendly
CITATION	Official document of praise
LEGITIMATE	Legal; lawful
EXALTED	Praiseworthy

CONCEITED	Having a very high opinion of oneself
SQUABBLED	Argued
OBSTACLES	Things that get in the way or stop progress
TAUT	Tense; tight
HOSTILE	Unfriendly; showing hatred toward another

RUCKSACK	Backpack
REMORSE	Strong feeling of guilt or sorrow
PUNCTURE	Reduce someone's confidence
ELATED	Happy and excited
SCARCE	In short or limited supply

TRAJECTORY	Route; path
OBSCENE	Morally offensive
EVACUATES	Leaves a dangerous place
GYPS	Cheats out of money
SECTOR	Zone; division

ANARCHIST	One who thinks government should be abandoned
SOCIALISTS	People who believe in control by the people
DORMER	Window built at right angles to the roof
PRY	Force apart or open with a lever
VAGUE	Not clear in meaning

EXHILARATION	Happiness and excitement
SCRUTINIZING	Examining carefully
AGITATORS	Protesters; troublemakers
CONTEMPTUOUSLY	In a disapproving way
INTERN	Put in prison

IMPARTIALLY	Fairly
BRITTLENESS	Being weak and likely to break or crack
FALLACY	Belief that is actually incorrect
CYNICISM	Negative sarcasm or mockery
DEVOUT	Very religious

SHEDS	Causes water to flow or drop off
GUSTS	Sudden, violent bursts of wind
BILE	Fluid produced in the liver
GROGGY	Weak or dizzy; not fully alert
CHALET	Traditional Swiss wooden cottage

INVIGORATING	Filling with energy
MATRONLY	Like a mature woman with sensible qualities
NUISANCE	Annoyance; irritation
DISMAL	Gloomy; depressing
TORRENT	Fast, powerful flood of water

UNGAINLY	Clumsy; not graceful
PROTRACTED	Lasting for a long time
STRAINED	Full of tension; nervous

Farewell To Arms Vocabulary

AGITATORS	REMORSE	CAMIONS	ELATED	COAGULATES
ANARCHIST	BELLOWS	VAGUE	FRAGMENTS	CYNICISM
ATHEISTS	EXHILARATION	FREE SPACE	PRY	OBSTACLES
EMERY	REFRAINED	OBSCENE	COMMENCED	PORTER
SENTIMENT	SQUABBLED	CORDIAL	UNCHAPERONED	TRUSS

Farewell To Arms Vocabulary

ARTICULATION	CHOLERA	DRESSING	SECTOR	SOCIALISTS
SCARCE	FALLACY	DECORATED	PROTRACTED	CONSCIENTIOUSLY
CITATION	DORMER	FREE SPACE	DISMAL	BATTERY
RUPTURE	TRAJECTORY	EXALTED	DEVOUT	ARTILLERY
OFFENSIVE	CONTEMPTUOUSLY	INFANTRY	TAUT	NUISANCE

Farewell To Arms Vocabulary

RUPTURE	BATTERY	INVIGORATING	OBSTACLES	DISMAL
DORMER	CONSCIENTIOUSLY	ARTILLERY	DRESSING	ANARCHIST
SOCIALISTS	TRUSS	FREE SPACE	SENTIMENT	VAGUE
FALLACY	SOLEMN	COAGULATES	CONTEMPTUOUSLY	OFFENSIVE
ARTICULATION	COMMENCED	TAUT	TRAJECTORY	EMERY

Farewell To Arms Vocabulary

TORRENT	DOMINEERING	STRAINED	SCARCE	FRAGMENTS
RIDGE	PORTER	FORMALITIES	CYNICISM	CAMIONS
IMPARTIALLY	ELATED	FREE SPACE	BILE	CITATION
PUNCTURE	EXHILARATION	ATHEISTS	REMORSE	PROJECTILE
TOURNIQUET	DEVOUT	EVACUATES	GROGGY	HEMORRHAGE

Farewell To Arms Vocabulary

ARTILLERY	DISMAL	GUSTS	SOCIALISTS	EVACUATES
TRUSS	SENTIMENT	HOSTILE	SCRUTINIZING	STRAINED
CHOLERA	RIDGE	FREE SPACE	FRAGMENTS	INVIGORATING
INTERN	IMPARTIALLY	BILE	EXALTED	UNCHAPERONED
SOLEMN	ANARCHIST	PROTRACTED	OFFENSIVE	FORMALITIES

Farewell To Arms Vocabulary

ELATED	LEGITIMATE	SCARCE	PROJECTILE	DRESSING
REGIMENT	TORRENT	CORDIAL	GYPS	DORMER
GROGGY	ATHEISTS	FREE SPACE	CONSCIENTIOUSLY	UNGAINLY
PRY	TAUT	CITATION	TRAJECTORY	BRITTLENESS
CAMIONS	OBSTACLES	CYNICISM	RUCKSACK	COMMENCED

Farewell To Arms Vocabulary

COAGULATES	BATTERY	DORMER	SHEDS	EXHILARATION
REGIMENT	RUPTURE	ANARCHIST	SECTOR	DECORATED
TAUT	BELLOWS	FREE SPACE	BRITTLENESS	FRAGMENTS
EMERY	TRAJECTORY	CHALET	MATRONLY	DOMINEERING
RIDGE	INFANTRY	CAMIONS	DISMAL	CORDIAL

Farewell To Arms Vocabulary

SQUABBLED	CYNICISM	AGITATORS	GUSTS	HOSTILE
NUISANCE	FORMALITIES	INVIGORATING	ATHEISTS	PRY
TOURNIQUET	REFRAINED	FREE SPACE	ELATED	UNCHAPERONED
DRESSING	BILE	CITATION	HEMORRHAGE	CONTEMPTUOUSLY
EXALTED	PROJECTILE	IMPARTIALLY	LEGITIMATE	OBSTACLES

Farewell To Arms Vocabulary

CYNICISM	SENTIMENT	DISMAL	TRAJECTORY	BRITTLENESS
PORTER	PUNCTURE	TOURNIQUET	INFANTRY	CONSCIENTIOUSLY
DECORATED	GROGGY	FREE SPACE	INTERN	SCARCE
DOMINEERING	DRESSING	ANARCHIST	SHEDS	AGITATORS
COMMENCED	TAUT	FRAGMENTS	REGIMENT	DORMER

Farewell To Arms Vocabulary

VAGUE	CORDIAL	CHOLERA	MATRONLY	PROTRACTED
BILE	FALLACY	ARTILLERY	TORRENT	ATHEISTS
SOLEMN	HOSTILE	FREE SPACE	SOCIALISTS	BATTERY
PRY	RUPTURE	CONCEITED	CONTEMPTUOUSLY	SECTOR
DEVOUT	RUCKSACK	PROJECTILE	IMPARTIALLY	REMORSE

Farewell To Arms Vocabulary

EMERY	OBSCENE	RUPTURE	PUNCTURE	INVIGORATING
CONSCIENTIOUSLY	ANARCHIST	SOLEMN	CONTEMPTUOUSLY	PORTER
DORMER	DEVOUT	FREE SPACE	REFRAINED	AGITATORS
INFANTRY	SQUABBLED	CHALET	EXALTED	MATRONLY
CITATION	OBSTACLES	NUISANCE	SCRUTINIZING	SCARCE

Farewell To Arms Vocabulary

CYNICISM	SENTIMENT	PROJECTILE	ARTILLERY	BRITTLENESS
CHOLERA	UNCHAPERONED	UNGAINLY	ELATED	TORRENT
REMORSE	DRESSING	FREE SPACE	SOCIALISTS	BILE
COAGULATES	CONCEITED	BATTERY	DOMINEERING	TOURNIQUET
GUSTS	LEGITIMATE	ATHEISTS	DISMAL	VAGUE

Farewell To Arms Vocabulary

ATHEISTS	CHOLERA	SCARCE	SOLEMN	NUISANCE
PUNCTURE	DECORATED	FRONT	DEVOUT	SQUABBLED
STRAINED	RUCKSACK	FREE SPACE	EXHILARATION	CITATION
ARTICULATION	PRY	BATTERY	CONCEITED	CONSCIENTIOUSLY
TORRENT	RUPTURE	OBSTACLES	INVIGORATING	TOURNIQUET

Farewell To Arms Vocabulary

FALLACY	SOCIALISTS	DISMAL	TRAJECTORY	CHALET
EVACUATES	PROTRACTED	EXALTED	REMORSE	UNGAINLY
INFANTRY	HOSTILE	FREE SPACE	SENTIMENT	BELLOWS
MATRONLY	ARTILLERY	REGIMENT	ANARCHIST	AGITATORS
HEMORRHAGE	COMMENCED	SECTOR	EMERY	GROGGY

Farewell To Arms Vocabulary

DORMER	PORTER	ARTICULATION	INTERN	EVACUATES
BILE	CYNICISM	FRONT	DOMINEERING	TRUSS
REFRAINED	AGITATORS	FREE SPACE	CORDIAL	REMORSE
FORMALITIES	SCRUTINIZING	HOSTILE	DISMAL	RUPTURE
CONSCIENTIOUSLY	CONTEMPTUOUSLY	ANARCHIST	DEVOUT	TOURNIQUET

Farewell To Arms Vocabulary

PRY	NUISANCE	PROTRACTED	SOCIALISTS	REGIMENT
TAUT	CHOLERA	LEGITIMATE	BATTERY	RIDGE
SCARCE	PROJECTILE	FREE SPACE	VAGUE	GROGGY
SQUABBLED	COMMENCED	DRESSING	BELLOWS	ATHEISTS
TRAJECTORY	IMPARTIALLY	ELATED	UNGAINLY	CHALET

Farewell To Arms Vocabulary

RIDGE	BILE	COAGULATES	DOMINEERING	DECORATED
HOSTILE	BATTERY	REFRAINED	TRUSS	LEGITIMATE
CAMIONS	REMORSE	FREE SPACE	SQUABBLED	INVIGORATING
CONTEMPTUOUSLY	SCARCE	SECTOR	TAUT	SOLEMN
OFFENSIVE	DRESSING	UNGAINLY	CYNICISM	SHEDS

Farewell To Arms Vocabulary

BELLOWS	RUCKSACK	CHALET	SOCIALISTS	DISMAL
NUISANCE	EXHILARATION	BRITTLENESS	RUPTURE	PROTRACTED
FRAGMENTS	EXALTED	FREE SPACE	SENTIMENT	ANARCHIST
TORRENT	CITATION	FALLACY	IMPARTIALLY	CONCEITED
FORMALITIES	ARTICULATION	VAGUE	CONSCIENTIOUSLY	REGIMENT

Farewell To Arms Vocabulary

DISMAL	INVIGORATING	RUCKSACK	OBSCENE	INFANTRY
FALLACY	HEMORRHAGE	GROGGY	OFFENSIVE	LEGITIMATE
EXHILARATION	SENTIMENT	FREE SPACE	IMPARTIALLY	BATTERY
SECTOR	RIDGE	EVACUATES	BELLOWS	GUSTS
TAUT	PUNCTURE	BILE	CONTEMPTUOUSLY	DRESSING

Farewell To Arms Vocabulary

PROTRACTED	DEVOUT	REMORSE	ARTICULATION	DECORATED
UNGAINLY	INTERN	REFRAINED	VAGUE	CONCEITED
ARTILLERY	AGITATORS	FREE SPACE	SCRUTINIZING	SCARCE
NUISANCE	TORRENT	BRITTLENESS	SHEDS	CAMIONS
FRONT	SQUABBLED	CORDIAL	SOLEMN	CITATION

Farewell To Arms Vocabulary

VAGUE	CONCEITED	FRAGMENTS	IMPARTIALLY	EVACUATES
UNCHAPERONED	TRUSS	FRONT	COMMENCED	DECORATED
GYPS	BILE	FREE SPACE	PORTER	DOMINEERING
CHOLERA	SOLEMN	RUPTURE	DEVOUT	TRAJECTORY
CONSCIENTIOUSLY	REGIMENT	SQUABBLED	UNGAINLY	DRESSING

Farewell To Arms Vocabulary

REMORSE	TOURNIQUET	GUSTS	SCRUTINIZING	SOCIALISTS
GROGGY	SECTOR	HEMORRHAGE	TORRENT	BELLOWS
FALLACY	SHEDS	FREE SPACE	BATTERY	FORMALITIES
CYNICISM	PRY	EXHILARATION	EXALTED	LEGITIMATE
PROTRACTED	ANARCHIST	OBSTACLES	AGITATORS	DISMAL

Farewell To Arms Vocabulary

CAMIONS	GUSTS	AGITATORS	BELLOWS	OBSCENE
SHEDS	FRONT	TRAJECTORY	SCARCE	INVIGORATING
EVACUATES	SENTIMENT	FREE SPACE	OFFENSIVE	PUNCTURE
ELATED	TAUT	RIDGE	PRY	DECORATED
COAGULATES	OBSTACLES	DORMER	FORMALITIES	HOSTILE

Farewell To Arms Vocabulary

DEVOUT	TOURNIQUET	EXALTED	FRAGMENTS	GYPS
BRITTLENESS	STRAINED	CORDIAL	PORTER	TORRENT
REMORSE	INFANTRY	FREE SPACE	PROTRACTED	HEMORRHAGE
DISMAL	CYNICISM	EXHILARATION	ARTILLERY	PROJECTILE
REGIMENT	ATHEISTS	TRUSS	CHALET	BATTERY

Farewell To Arms Vocabulary

RUPTURE	COMMENCED	UNGAINLY	PRY	GUSTS
EMERY	INVIGORATING	IMPARTIALLY	SCRUTINIZING	PORTER
SOLEMN	MATRONLY	FREE SPACE	DOMINEERING	SHEDS
TRAJECTORY	FORMALITIES	HEMORRHAGE	CONSCIENTIOUSLY	BATTERY
SQUABBLED	DORMER	CHOLERA	SCARCE	HOSTILE

Farewell To Arms Vocabulary

RIDGE	COAGULATES	GROGGY	REGIMENT	CITATION
CONTEMPTUOUSLY	TORRENT	OBSCENE	ARTILLERY	OBSTACLES
ATHEISTS	FRAGMENTS	FREE SPACE	DEVOUT	NUISANCE
SENTIMENT	REMORSE	DECORATED	ELATED	BELLOWS
EXALTED	PROTRACTED	ANARCHIST	GYPS	FALLACY

Farewell To Arms Vocabulary

TRAJECTORY	SENTIMENT	PROTRACTED	OFFENSIVE	RUCKSACK
FRAGMENTS	FRONT	FALLACY	INFANTRY	UNCHAPERONED
TAUT	HEMORRHAGE	FREE SPACE	PROJECTILE	EVACUATES
CHOLERA	NUISANCE	DEVOUT	STRAINED	BILE
BATTERY	DECORATED	TORRENT	TOURNIQUET	SHEDS

Farewell To Arms Vocabulary

SOLEMN	COMMENCED	DORMER	CONCEITED	LEGITIMATE
SECTOR	ELATED	CORDIAL	GYPS	REGIMENT
MATRONLY	TRUSS	FREE SPACE	FORMALITIES	ARTICULATION
HOSTILE	ANARCHIST	ARTILLERY	OBSCENE	DOMINEERING
RIDGE	CHALET	RUPTURE	AGITATORS	EXALTED

Farewell To Arms Vocabulary

PROTRACTED	OBSCENE	OFFENSIVE	CITATION	FRAGMENTS
CHOLERA	GROGGY	OBSTACLES	DISMAL	PORTER
SOLEMN	IMPARTIALLY	FREE SPACE	INFANTRY	REGIMENT
DEVOUT	TORRENT	CONTEMPTUOUSLY	BRITTLENESS	MATRONLY
CYNICISM	TRUSS	CHALET	CORDIAL	HEMORRHAGE

Farewell To Arms Vocabulary

STRAINED	DORMER	GUSTS	SECTOR	ANARCHIST
ARTICULATION	ELATED	RUCKSACK	DRESSING	CONCEITED
BILE	UNCHAPERONED	FREE SPACE	BATTERY	PROJECTILE
COMMENCED	INVIGORATING	HOSTILE	EVACUATES	AGITATORS
INTERN	SENTIMENT	EXALTED	DECORATED	SOCIALISTS

Farewell To Arms Vocabulary

REFRAINED	DECORATED	SECTOR	HOSTILE	INVIGORATING
TOURNIQUET	TORRENT	TAUT	DOMINEERING	SHEDS
ARTICULATION	PUNCTURE	FREE SPACE	EXALTED	RIDGE
FRONT	RUCKSACK	AGITATORS	INTERN	NUISANCE
ANARCHIST	EXHILARATION	GROGGY	CAMIONS	UNGAINLY

Farewell To Arms Vocabulary

CYNICISM	STRAINED	DEVOUT	TRUSS	OBSTACLES
REGIMENT	ATHEISTS	TRAJECTORY	OBSCENE	SENTIMENT
CITATION	SCRUTINIZING	FREE SPACE	PROJECTILE	LEGITIMATE
IMPARTIALLY	UNCHAPERONED	FORMALITIES	GYPS	OFFENSIVE
SOCIALISTS	HEMORRHAGE	DORMER	CONCEITED	PORTER